6

The
Golden
Strings

The Golden Strings

by

True Davidson

GRIFFIN HOUSE
TORONTO ·1973

ISBN 0 88760 067 0

Published by Griffin Press Limited
455 King Street West, Toronto M5V 1K7 Canada

Printed in Canada

To my Father

Misunderstood and lonely
    Almost to the end,
Your courage never faltered,
    Your will knew not to bend.

Pity you learned and patience
    Beyond all grief or mirth,
And your love was rooted deeply
    As a tree in ancient earth.

You found a sweet solution
    For frustrate human pain,
And your faith was clean and quiet
    As grass after rain.

"They came—they came to Jesus,"
    On fevered bed you sighed,
"They found Him, and they tried it;
    "It worked," you said, and died.

You took all false ambition
    And pride and fear from me;
You took the fence I leaned on
    And somehow set me free.

Out of your faith and courage
    Your child was born anew;
All I have done, my father,
    Since then, I owe to you.

Contents

Prologue   Of Time and Death / 3

Chapter 1   The Seeker   *Wilder Penfield* / 8

2   The Indomitable   *John Diefenbaker* / 18

3   The Happy Warrior   *Nathan Phillips* / 27

4   The Gentle Heroine   *Thérèse Casgrain* / 35

5   The Life Force   *Vida Peene* / 48

6   The Bulldozer   *Fred Gardiner* / 55

7   The Traders   *Oakah Jones & Roy Britnell* / 60

8   Prince of the Church   *Paul-Emile Leger* / 70

9   The Woodsman   *Roy Ivor* / 81

10   The Recreationists   *Harry & Helen Mole* / 88

11   The Creative Artist   *A. Y. Jackson* / 93

12   The Enthusiasts   *Richard Jones & Gordon Bates* / 103

13   The Reformer   *David Croll* / 110

14   The Healers   *Robert McClure & Lavell Smith* / 118

15   The Mother   *Pauline Vanier* / 127

16   The Wise Man   *Dan George* / 134

17   The Interpreter   *Hugh MacLennan* / 141

Epilogue   The Gate / 152

Footnotes   / 157

FREDERICK G. GARDINER, Q.C., fishing with Miss Outdoors (Nancy Robson) at the Glen Haffy Conservation Area Official Opening. Mr. Gardiner is still interested in the Conservation authority and has often appeared at official functions.

HON. THERESE-F. CASGRAIN, leaning from a truck to hand a leaflet to a worker during a political campaign.

(Canadian Opera Company and Walter Graham)
MISS VIDA HAMPT PEENE, S.M., chatting with Dr. Herman Geiger-Torel, General Director of the Canadian Opera Company.

RT. HON. JOHN G. DIEFENBAKER (centre) shaking hands with Leslie Frost, former Premier of Ontario, at the time of the Diefenbaker sweep in 1958. Looking on is Willis L. Blair, present mayor of East York.

(The Toronto Sun)

DR. WILDER PENFIELD, talks about the
problem under review.

PAUL-EMILE CARDINAL LEGER, holding one of the African babies with whose
care he concerns himself.

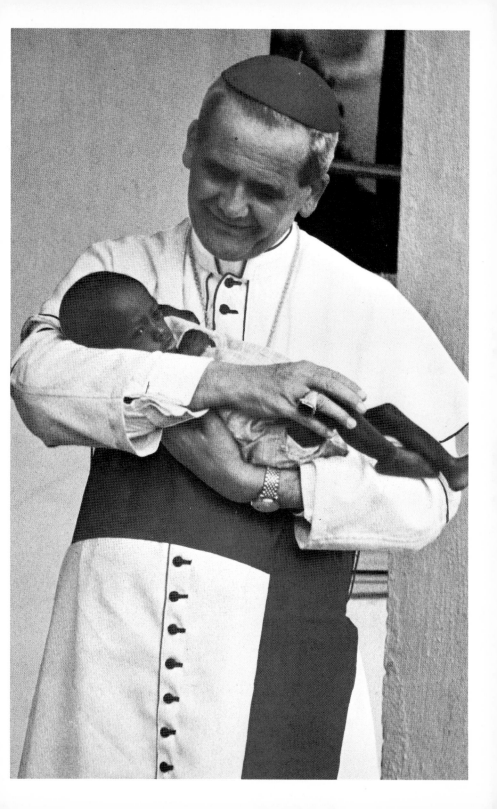

ROY BRITNELL, briefing a sales assistant
on a new book.

(The Toronto Sun)

ROY IVOR and a feathered friend who is
being pampered.

(Turofsky)

HIS WORSHIP MAYOR NATHAN PHIL-
LIPS, escorting Her Majesty Queen Elizabeth
II on the occasion of a gala civic reception,
June 18th, 1959.

ALEXANDER YOUNG JACKSON, C.C.,
C.M.G., LL.D., still happy at ninety with
his brushes, his paints, and his books.

DR. GORDON BATES, receiving his O.C.
from the Governor-General, His Excellency,
the Rt. Hon. Roland Michener.

HARRY MOLE, with his arm around his wife HELEN, and giving the other to the author, then Mayor of East York.

REV. RICHARD JONES, giving a sales pitch to Prime Minister Trudeau.

(The Toronto Sun)

MADAME GEORGES-P. VANIER, C.C.,
P.C., receiving a bouquet of flowers, meets
the little donor on her own level.

DR. ROBERT McCLURE, One of the world's great healers of both soul and body.

CHIEF DAN GEORGE, makes his point strongly in dramatic contrast with the mild and benevolent tone he more frequently uses.

SENATOR DAVID CROLL, with unwont-
edly tidy hair; the reader should have seen
him at the poverty hearing.

HUGH MacLENNAN, author and professor, alone with his typewriter and his
thoughts.

OAKAH JONES, wearing his C.N.E. blazer, talks to a couple of midget baseballers, part of his programme of meeting the people.

DR. J. LAVELL SMITH, with a group of boys from downtown Toronto. Taken at Lake Scugog Camp.

The
Golden
Strings

Of Time and Death

Time

"Run," says Time, cracking his whip,
Time, the lean sadist with hungry talons and eyes where ancient lava
      smoulders.

We rush blindly, fall headlong when we trip,
Scramble to our feet again, and leap forward, quivering.
What we are to do, get, be, doesn't matter.
As the whip curls greedily about our shrinking shoulders
We are surrounded by claptrap and clatter
And over it all his sardonic laughter.

"I am catching up on you," he shrills. "Slaves, be about your slavery."

The ground is stony and we stumble; it is wet and treacherous and
      we slip;
The faster we run, the faster he seems to follow after
And we cannot avoid the whip.

We hurry from an urgency we do not understand to a horror we have
      not yet experienced,
With a sense of ever-imminent doom, of the eyes of judge, prosecutor
      and spy peering at us.
Yet is it not possible that we carry him with us, as brute beasts
      drawing a chariot
In which our taskmaster rides, goading us onward, taunting us,
      jeering at us,

3

Shouting, "Hurry, hurry! I am close at your heels;
"There is a better speed than that, a stronger endeavour;
"Hurry, though the heart ticks doom like a hidden bomb, red mist
          blinds the eyes and the brain reels;
"If you stop a moment to rest I am on you, cutting you down like
          juggernaut,
"Leaving you broken behind in silence for ever and ever.
"I am the devil you feared and ran away from, the god you vainly
          sought."

He should not have said *for ever*—
Not Time, and not to men.
We think; we ask questions, and that is what makes us what we are.

If we stopped running, would we not also stop his car,
Stop the wheels that keep turning and turning?
If we could be done with joy and pain, with all the fearing and
          yearning,
If we dared to sever
The traces,
If we refused to scurry frantically faster and faster,
Not asking whither or where,
As if bigger were better, and faster more fine and fair,
If we stood and let the quiet of eternity again
Flow into our hearts and over our faces,
Silence and wisdom following the glib dexterity of the verbal chime,
Would we not be
Free from the wheel and the whip for ever and ever and ever?

Man was not meant to be the slave of the work of his own hands or
          the measure of his days, but their master;
When he finds the truth, the truth shall make him free.

Prologue

I lay on a sleepless bed and thought of time and eternity, life and death. Fragments of old verse drifted through my memory:

> "I saw Eternity the other night
> "Like a great ring of pure and endless light."[1]

> "Life, like a dome of many-coloured glass,
> Stains the white radiance of eternity."[2]

> "Time, like an ever-rolling stream,
> Bears all its sons away."[3]

> "From too much love of living,
> From hope and fear set free,
> We thank, with brief thanksgiving,
> Whatever gods may be,
> That no life lives for ever,
> That dead men rise up never,
> That even the weariest river
> Winds somewhere safe to sea."[4]

> "O degenerate sons and daughters,
> It takes life to love life."[5]

> "A thousand ages in Thy sight
> are but as yesterday when it has passed
> or as a watch in the night."[6]

> "I came that ye might have life
> and that ye might have it more abundantly."[7]

But those last two are not just poetry. They are part of the Word, in the light of which all mere words are significant or are nothing.

And so I ask myself: What is this more abundant life which Jesus came to bring mankind? This life which makes Time irrelevant, and death a part of life?

It is not length of days as measured by the movements of the stars.

In the blazing light of the universe, all human history and pre-history is like The Lord's Prayer written on the head of a pin.

Nor is it the brief brilliance of a decade or two, and then the slowly dying ash of old age; only a bitter irony could call this abundant life. It must be a question of quality, not quantity, but the quality must be consistent.

Why do some retired people turn into merely tired people? Why do so many fritter away their days in endless games of euchre or bingo, or in pathetically inconsequential chatter about the past? Why do others, with more energy and drive, spend it on constant niggling demands for increased pensions and benefits and more free entertainment? While others can never find enough moments for all they still wish to learn and understand and do?

The problems of youth are often agonizing. I remember mine as if I had encountered them yesterday. Is it because so much of our so-called civilization is awry that many of us suffer so much in learning to live, even when those who love us would give their lives to spare us pain? All younger people are to me as children or grandchildren, whom it is my privilege to love and try to understand. I do not discount their misgivings and disillusionments.

But I am growing old. I am half blind and no longer balance well. I was told a decade ago not to try any longer to swim or skate or dance. I do not suppose I could do so now if I tried. But my spirit—the essential me—is still as full of wonder and delight as that of a young girl. I do not want to become a placid observer on the banks of the stream. I want to stay in the current, thrill to the full pressure of life, until death sweeps me over the falls. I do not want to cling abjectly to this bodily existence "as though to breathe were life."[8] I am not afraid of what lies over the falls. But while I am still in the river of time I want to pull at least my own weight in the boat.

What makes the difference between those who can and those who cannot, I ask myself. I think of my grandparents, my parents, teachers and employers. I think of my classmates of 2T1 Victoria, of people I have worked with professionally or politically or in those extra-curricular activities which are often the richest of our associations. I fancy I see a thread of connection. Perhaps I have the end of William Blake's "golden string" which, rolled into a ball, should lead us into "heaven's gate built in Jerusalem's wall."

By this time all desire for sleep has left me. I am wildly excited. I go to my study, seeking confirmation in the printed word of what my observations and intuitions suggest. The hours run into days and weeks, and take me to the public libraries and bookstores.

Of course, I can read only about those who are personally articulate or who have caught the attention of the articulate. But I am amazed to find how many times my original intuition about these outstanding men and women seems to be borne out more and more strongly by each additional approach.

Perhaps I find in the stories of their lives just what I am looking for—I'm afraid many researchers do this—and if there are finer and greater aspects that I have missed, I am sorry. I do not pretend to be writing biographies, or even making thumbnail sketches. I am seeking exemplars.

Nor do I mean to suggest that only great men and women can live abundantly. If I take them as my texts it is because their names are familiar. I could have chosen a far larger number who are almost unknown outside the group or groups in which I have known them, but in those groups are a source of inspiration and strength. They are part of my personal golden string.

And because I am, myself, a Seeker on this Quest, I turn first to Dr. Wilder Penfield, a man who has for some time stood out in my mind as one who sought both knowledge and understanding.

Evolution

The sky of marble blue and grey
The black sea-waves, the white sea-spray,
These are the things that will abide
After the wind, after the tide.

Ice ages follow births in flame,
But nature's laws remain the same;
Defeat and triumph leave behind
The ever-urgent human mind.

From *Muses of the Modern Day*

The Seeker 1

Education

What can you be told
In a hundred words or so
That you will grasp and hold
As you move along and grow?

Education is what remains
When all that you have learned
From the printed page alone,
Dust in your tired brains,
Is dead as the leaves blown
By the autumn wind and burned.

The habit of taking pains
To get the job done right,
The will to understand,
The will to fight,
And then the friendly hand,
The passion to know and be known,
Courage to walk alone
And never swerve,
The love of truth,
The will to serve, —
These are the soil your roots deserve,
O tree of youth.

From the first issue of *The Cosburn Comet*

Dr. Wilder Penfield

When he was seventy-one, Dr. Wilder Graves Penfield, first director of the Montreal Neurological Institute, and still its honorary consultant, ended his contribution to a symposium at the University of Melbourne on the soaring note of a young graduate:

> "Beware, then, of the great social disease, the closure of the windows of the mind, the loneliness of selfish solitude, the isolation that limits achievement for many specialists. Welcome the wind from the Ocean of Truth. Walk on its shores and be content to pick up the pebbles you find, listening there for the whisper of wisdom for every man."

Dr. Penfield has lived by his own prescription, and perhaps that is one of the reasons he has lived to ripeness and accomplished so much. His public utterances show wide reading in poetry and philosophic prose and the highest concepts of spiritual reality. He published two novels after he had reached what many would consider retirement age; both are based on painstaking research, and work on both was crowded into the crevices of a busy professional life. He has been persistent, but not rigid; responsive to winds and currents, but always setting his course by his own stars.

Born in the United States on the 26th of January, 1891, Wilder Penfield seems to have had the seeds of success in him from the beginning. Whatever he undertook seemed to prosper. Yet he was not beguiled into a premature determination of his destiny.

At Princeton he reached the summit of many a boy's ambition, as a successful footballer and coach, but he did not become a professional athlete.

As a Rhodes scholar at Oxford, he studied physiology under Sir Charles Sherrington, himself a man of long vitality and a Nobel prizewinner at the age of 75; but did not stay in England even to use all his scholarship time. He finished his work at Johns Hopkins, in Baltimore, and interned in Boston where he had a chance to watch the great surgeon, Harvey Cushing.

His destiny now seemed clearer. He must open new avenues in the fields of neurosurgery, neuropathology and neurophysiology. He must explore, as fully as his years and faculties should permit, that part of man which is most closely integrated with his humanness, and any failure in which is most tragic. He returned to Oxford for post-graduate work.

Later, in London at the Queen Square Hospital for "the paralyzed and the epileptic",[9] he had a chance to study the actual pathology and anatomy of the human brain, a "rewarding experience" though he was not completely satisfied with the method in use for preparing pathological slides.

When he returned to New York, loaded with debt, he was taken on at the Presbyterian Hospital, and at Columbia University. Here, too, he sought better methods. He secured six months' leave to study in Spain with Ramon y Cajal, a Nobel prize-winner of 1906, still "carrying his seventy-odd years lightly",[10] and with his pupil del-Rio Hortega.

During the next few years, while working very hard with a young assistant, in his new Laboratory of Neurocytology, Dr. Penfield still found time to work on a project which was amazing in several ways. The concept was daring—almost audacious for a comparatively young man, so early in his career, and with limited facilities—an "exhaustive book on neurological pathology with the help of the Spanish methods".[11] It is even more surprising—though not in view of the character of the man—that he proceeded so systematically to the execution of the project. Most amazing of all, he did not allow the current of all this focussed energy within himself to sweep him entirely away from objective moorings. He soon realized that he would destroy the whole project if he tried to keep it to himself and his young partner. There were men in Chicago, Boston, Madrid, London, Paris, Munich and Berlin, who could do certain parts of the work better than he, and he had the courage and intellectual honesty to shift his own position to that of editor and contributor, and the skill and charm to seek, and eventually obtain, the co-operation of men some of whom at that time were better known and more dis-tinguished than himself.

While this project was still under way, Dr. Penfield accepted a position in Montreal in connection with the McGill University School of Medicine. Perhaps he instinctively felt that he would have a freer hand there, and more opportunity to follow the methods and ideas he had worked out for himself, rather than accepting a safer but perhaps less challenging opening in a large and expanding American institution. I have also wondered if he was influenced, subconsciously

10

no doubt, by the possibility of getting another six months in Europe between jobs.

This time he spent chiefly with Otfried Foerster in Breslau, Germany, who had done twelve operations on sufferers from epilepsy similar to one Dr. Penfield had performed in Presbyterian Hospital in New York.

Back in Canada he immediately began to seek funds for the service he hoped to develop. Naturally he thought of the Rockefeller Foundation which was active everywhere, and which was broadening its medical division. Rejected once, he was not discouraged. He applied again, and Sir Arthur Currie, the vice-chancellor of McGill, telephoned New York to support the request. Eventually Alan Gregg, the new director of the division, decided to visit Montreal and size up the situation for himself.

By the time Gregg arrived, Penfield's little monograph on "The Cytology and Cellular Pathology of the Nervous System" had grown into three massive volumes. Furthermore, it was in the hands of the publishers.

It is obvious that Gregg and Penfield found each other congenial. Both were young at heart, just at the beginning of new careers, only six months apart in age. The latter was seeking aid for his most ambitious project to date; he was frank in his statement of need. However, he sought no clever prepared stances to impress a visitor who might be more conservative than himself. He was amusingly honest. Indeed he records that "Gregg was highly amused by his arbitrary division of these men (distinguished Europeans working with the brain and nervous system) into two groups: Authoritarians —men with closed minds; and Honest Teachers—those with open minds, who were ready to listen to the young."[12] Neither Wilder Penfield nor Alan Gregg was ever destined to become an Authoritarian.

The Rockefeller Foundation was always looking, according to Gregg, "for the man with a 'germinal idea'."[13] Trying to find such a man was like gambling on a horse race. You did the best you could from the reviewing stand. But if you wanted to give really wisely, you should also try to understand "the horse's eye view of the world," since it is only so that you can judge "the heart, the speed, and the staying power of each contestant".[14] They talked long and frankly and Gregg was convinced.

The grant to the Montreal Neurological Institute was approved in

April, 1932. The Institute was opened in 1934, and in that same year Wilder Penfield became a Canadian citizen. He had found his destiny.

But that did not close the windows of his mind. If it had, he would not have been the Wilder Penfield so many, both inside and outside Canada, so greatly admire. And I would certainly not have thought of him first among these with heart, speed and staying power to give me a suitable springboard for my initial leap.

At that time my knowledge of Dr. Penfield could have been written on one page of a stenographer's notebook, except for one fact: I had read his novel, "No Other Gods". Indeed I possessed a copy, which I had read twice.

Perhaps it is not a great novel; the people and dialogue are both a bit stiff; one doesn't suffer with them, doesn't share their wonder and joy. Yet I had felt a quality in the book which is hard to analyze. On the second reading I had decided that the author was more than a great neurosurgeon and neuropathologist. He was a great lover of truth, a seeker of wisdom. I had laid the book aside, instead of passing it on, as I have been doing for years with most fiction. And when I sought for the end of my golden string I found it here.

Since I chose him as my prototype of the Seeker, I have read all I could find of his non-technical published work, and my intuition has been confirmed a thousandfold.

My delight culminated in the last book I read—a tiny one the East York Public Library had some difficulty in getting for me. It was worth waiting for because it indicates one of Dr. Penfield's own second careers. It is called "Man and his Family" and I shall be saying something more about it when I refer directly to Madame Vanier as the type of the Mother. It is a transcript of the Josiah Wood Lecture given by Dr. Penfield to Mount Allison University in Sackville, N.S., and there is a Foreword by the late Governor-General of Canada, General Georges-P. Vanier.

In his foreword, His Excellency referred to a Conference on the Family which he and Madame Vanier had gathered on June 7, 1964. At that conference they assembled many of the most prominent social and religious workers and scholars.

The result was the Vanier Institute of the Family. At the age of seventy-three Dr. Penfield accepted the presidency of this completely new undertaking for research and service,—an undertaking which in 1967, in closing "Man and his Family", he was to call "the most important of my life's adventures."

Life had prepared him well for this. His novels, his historical and archaeological research and his writing on all sorts of general topics had kept the windows of his mind open when success in his chosen field might have encouraged a lesser man to a narrowed concentration which would have killed youthful resilience.

His novel "The Torch" is an imaginative reconstruction of the life of Hippocrates, whose passion for truth and dedication to his profession are commemorated in the Hippocratic Oath. Like "No Other Gods", it is based on extensive reading in history and archeology of a sort attractive only to a professional or one with an insatiable thirst for an understanding of man.

"The Difficult Art of Giving: The Epic of Alan Gregg" is perfectly suited to Dr. Penfield's literary talent, and is warmed by what is obviously a personal love for his subject. It reveals Dr. Penfield's own life and ideals as well as those of his friend.

To anyone like myself, however, trying to identify the sources of Dr. Penfield's enduring strength, the most exciting of his works is perhaps the slim volume of addresses and essays published as "The Second Career." His generous praise of outstanding men in his own and allied fields, and the qualities he singles out in them, are an indication of the wide variety of activities and interests he considers a part of the full life. His faith in the common man is equally delightful; although he draws his examples of second careers from famous people known to us all, he stresses the general application of what he has to say.

This essay on second careers is so encouraging to those who, like myself, have felt they were working with their left hands through most of their adult lives, that I cannot resist giving it special attention here. Dr. Penfield begins by quoting the late Sir William Osler, who said at his farewell dinner when he left Johns Hopkins at the age of 56:

"I have two fixed ideas. The first is the comparative uselessness of men above forty years of age. (He had been forty when he went to Baltimore.) . . . My second fixed idea is the uselessness of men above sixty years of age, and the incalculable benefit it would be in commercial, political and in professional life if, as a matter of course, men stopped work at this age."[15] There must have been some jocular reference to euthanasia, for people talked for some time about "Oslerizing" the aged, but this, he tried to point out was more "pleasantry". Apparently he maintained to the end, however, that "the effective, moving, vitalizing work of the world is done between the ages of 25 and 40."[16]

Dr. Penfield does not agree. He points out that Osler himself went on from Baltimore to an honoured career of fourteen years as Regius Professor of Medicine at Oxford, terminating only at the age of seventy. Indeed Osler's biographer, Harvey Cushing, then Professor of Surgery at Harvard, devoted to those years the entire second volume of his prize-winning biography.

Senescence, Penfield agrees, will come in time, but usually not until long after retirement at the age Osler suggested. "Consider," he says, "soldiers like Eisenhower and De Gaulle, who were pushed into second careers as statesmen. Challenge calls forth unsuspected greatness in the common man, and in the uncommon. Consider Clemenceau, Adenauer and Voltaire in their eighties; Verdi composing his greatest operas between seventy-four and eighty; Michelangelo painting the Last Judgment at sixty. Look at Winston Churchill. When he had reached the age of seventy-nine he was too busy to go to Stockholm to accept the Nobel Prize for work in the field of his second career, that of literature."[17] For such men, rest would have been rust.

Not all men are men of genius, but men of genius are after all merely men. We study them because we know or can find out more about them. But it is no truer of them than it is of the rest of us that if, "In our turbulent world, love and kindliness are man's most welcome blessings; work to good purpose (is) his most treasured privilege."[18]

Second careers work most successfully, I have observed, in cases where the foundation has already been laid for them during the prosecution of the major career, as with the writing of Winston Churchill or of Dr. Wilder himself. Many people feel, on retirement, that they could write a book "if they could only put their minds to it." If they have not felt the urge earlier, and acquired some of the skills with words, they will take no satisfaction in writing, any more than a man who had never worked on a farm or even had a garden could successfully undertake life on ten acres and his old age pension.

The man who has been able to use all of himself in his primary career will wish only to continue it. My Great-grandmother Grant, a centenarian, washed the dishes on her last day, I am told, sat in her old rocker by the kitchen window and quietly stopped breathing.

14

My Grandfather Davidson, in his nineties the last time I saw him, was setting in the sun with his cane beside him; he was gnarled and crippled by rheumatism, and had been doing less and less on the farm for some years, but he was still able to feel himself a part of the operation. Len Swain, works superintendent for East York, did not retire until he was seventy; we didn't know how to replace him, for he carried a wealth of knowledge of the *ad hoc* work done before the days of proper surveys and records, the bench-marks for which had disappeared: I missed him until the end of my term as mayor, and he still looks to me to be able to do a day's work with the best of the modern fat-boys who are more concerned with union negotiations and extra holidays than with accomplishment.

On the other hand, the factory lead hand whose garden has been his hobby, may undertake light work in a greenhouse, or seasonal maintenance of a bowling-green. The store clerk who really tried to please people, may become a hospital visitor or run the library in the children's home. The apartment-builder takes up the problem of preserving and improving the environment. Such people remain young longer than the rest of us and when they grow old they wither sweetly like russet apples or the black walnuts which can sometimes be found after years in an old farm attic, still sound and good.

All the essays in "The Second Career" are rich with revelations of Dr. Penfield's character. He was interested in education. His children had a German governess and the whole family acquired a smattering of Spanish before their six-month visit in Madrid. He has read widely, particularly in the poets, and supplies an apt quotation, as if by reflex action. His deep sense of the wonder and mystery of life, and his awareness of the God, Whom his hero, Abram, sought in the desert, among the marshes, and in the high places, are manifest again and again. His spontaneous admiration for quality and for achievement arises from a life too busy to be jealous or competitive.

He could almost qualify for a third career as a politician. In October, 1961, when he was nearly seventy-one, he offered a sound, constructive policy for governments in the atomic age, almost a new field for him, and yet a field for which he was well fitted by his medical background. "In the face of the possible extinction of society" he has the courage and common sense to advocate "an offensive of human understanding and friendship" in which both sides would be the winners, "an uprising of people who have no desire to proselyte and who are willing to discover that the philosophy and social system and religion on the other side suit their needs there as ours suit us . . . Somehow we must mobilize our spiritual strength."[19]

Knowledge and service to humanity: those are the twin aims of the "Honest Teacher". Dr. Penfield expressed the latter cogently in "Mankind in the Atomic Age." "Neurosurgery Yesterday, Today and Tomorrow" shows his passion for knowledge when he refers to the "alluring prospect of new discovery" as one of the chief attractions of his discipline. Calling poetry to the aid of prose exposition, as he so often does, he adds: "It is the call which explorers feel, I suppose, difficult to explain but powerful. Kipling called it an 'everlasting whisper'. 'Something hidden. Go and find it. Go and look behind the ranges—something lost behind the ranges. Lost and waiting for you. Go'."[20]

As long as the search is hot within him, the seeker cannot grow old.

Man

What is man? A predatory animal?
A bully? A killer? A looter?
A naked ape with a territorial imperative?
A piece of plastic material on an inexorable conveyor belt
Shaped by an inadequate and inadequately programmed computer?

Has anyone writing or speaking today
Anything positive and hopeful to say,
A sort of spiritual declarative
That will give
Something inside us that is deeper and higher a chance to live,
An "everlasting yea"
That's truly felt?

I have an "everlasting nay".
Man is not an animal like other animals.
There is fire in his heart
And he has taken fire in his hands.
He can do fifteen impossible things before breakfast
And believe fifty.
He is inquisitive and restless and shifty.
He makes all sorts of useful and useless, beautiful and ugly things
Because he is a maker,
But he is also a waster, a spoiler and a breaker,
Because being careful is too much bother.
He wishes on a star
And flies without wings,
And kills from afar.
He stands apart
From every other creature he has found in space.
He stands
And looks God in the face
And says, "My Father."

The
Indomitable 2

Land of Greatness

I used to walk on the prairies
    In the tangled, wild-flower spring,
With the wet wind sweet on my forehead
    And the migrant birds awing,
    And life was a wonderful thing.

        I used to walk on the prairies
            When the sun was a golden blaze,
        Wolf-willow a pungent silver,
            And the road a coppery haze
            Through long, laborious days.

I used to walk on the prairies
    When the straw-stacks were all on fire,
Through the chilly autumn darkness,
    As taut as a fine steel wire
    Vibrating with desire.

        I used to walk on the prairies
            When the year was ready to die
      And the snow seemed level and endless,
            But wherever you cast your eye
            The path reached into the sky.

I must go back to the prairies,
    For, whatever change I meet,
I must sense again the vastness
    Of those miles of cattle and wheat,
    Where earth and heaven meet.

Rt. Hon. John G. Diefenbaker

There have been greater Canadian statesmen than John George Diefenbaker: there have been more astute politicians. There have been few, if any, more commanding figures, and none more indomitable. If the motive power in the life of Dr. Wilder Penfield was intellectual and spiritual curiosity, John Diefenbaker's fuel was sheer raw courage.

He came of courageous stock. The Pennsylvania Dutch or Germans of Waterloo County were tough and hard-working. Many of them were of United Empire Loyalist extraction, with an ingrained horror of revolution. His mother's Scottish crofter ancestors had had three years with the Selkirk settlers at the Red River before returning to Ontario. In 1900 his own parents moved to the unincorporated village of Todmorden, in the township of York. There five-year-old John started school.

Todmorden at this time was little more than a post-office, a couple of churches, a rural school (S.D. No. 7, later Plains Road), and a handful of houses. A few mansions on Broadview Avenue spoke of former and future greatness, for Todmorden Mills had been the first industrial development outside the town of York, later Toronto. A lumber mill had been built there, by squatters perhaps, about the time Simcoe was choosing a site for the new capital of Upper Canada. Broadview Avenue went through in 1796 as the Mill Road, and Mrs. Simcoe speaks several times of the Skinners in her famous Diary.

The Skinners, Terrys and other Loyalists were reinforced in the early 1820's by Helliwells, Eastwoods and their workmen and dependents. All came from one Yorkshire town, and they gave its name to their new home. There were once some forty buildings in the valley alone, with many more on the tableland. But the replacement of water-power by steam, and several serious fires, not uncommon in those days of coal-oil lamps, combined to send most of the residents, and particularly the proprietors, to more promising locations, either in the city or in the township of Scarborough to the east of York.

However, the passionate loyalties of those who had been refugees and displaced persons from the Revolutionary War in the United States, and the pawky obstinacy of the Yorkshiremen, the love of both for church and king, their sturdy independence, and their pride in home, community and country, remained permanently imbedded

19

in the community they had founded, as flies in amber, immovable. It was in such a community, that young John Diefenbaker spent three of the most formative years of his early life. He attended the small rural school of which his father was principal, and the Todmorden Methodist Sunday-school (formerly Primitive Methodist). Young John had a head start on his school-fellows, as he had learned to read before starting school, but he had keen competition. East Yorkers still proudly cherish his record along with those of three schoolfellows who also became members of parliament, the Hon. R. H. McGregor, M.P., Joseph H. Harris, M.P., and George Tustin, M.P. A photograph of that famous class, faded and dim with age, still hangs in the centennial museum at Todmorden Mills, and we still regard John Diefenbaker as almost a native son.

I tried to get him to open the four-building historical complex for us this summer and his voice was as young and strong on the telephone as that of a man in the prime of life. We didn't get him—we've never managed yet to get him—but he named half a dozen people to whom he would like to be remembered. His "fellow Canadians", and when he says that it implies all that the warmest patriot would wish it to mean. He likes people, but he loves Canada, and he still feels that he has a mission to protect and preserve her.

Perhaps some of the indomitable character of John Diefenbaker, and some of his love of Canada too, spring from the hard days on the prairies. The Diefenbakers did not stay long in East York, much as we love to feel those few years made a lasting impression on young John's character. When he was eight years old his parents moved to the North-West Territories—the provinces of Saskatchewan and Alberta had not yet been organized.

I remember the old colonist cars by which they must have travelled, with hard wooden seats and a stove at the back of each car where you could heat something you had brought with you—we went west ourselves seven years later, and it was still a hard trip that my mother recalled for years as one her most exhausting experiences.

William Diefenbaker is remembered as a gentle man, deeply religious, a musician, a reader and thinker, and his piano or organ and books must have gone west with him, however small the shack to which they were going, and however humble with its wood stove and coal-oil lamps. Mrs. Diefenbaker, however, seems to have been the mainspring of action in the family, and was a continuing influence on the life of her elder son.

20

As Thomas Van Dusen points out in his fascinating book, "The Chief," Diefenbaker's dream of "One Canada" may well have been born in the tough life "on the prairie trails, in the fire and comradeship of World War I; in the section shacks of the railroad among immigrants with unpronounceable names; in the dreams of a new world free of prejudice and discrimination. . . . where every citizen enjoyed the same chance to get ahead, regardless of what part of the country he lived in, what his name might be, or where his parents had come from. . . . The spirit of the frontier was action; duty came first, and when the call came you answered. It was a school hardened by the savage temper of the weather. It called for self-reliance and dependence on one's own efforts; . . .remittance men, European noblemen (not all of them penniless), sodbusters, newly arrived immigrants, railroad builders, trappers, hunters and Mounted Police joined in the noble work of building a new frontier empire."[21] It was the world of Ralph Connor and Robert Service, stark and direct, where a man stood up to the worst that nature and fate could devise for him and stared it down.

They had some testing times in store for young John Diefenbaker. Impressed by reading a life of Laurier, the boy is said to have looked up from his book and said, "I'm going to be premier of Canada some day." But Laurier's charm and old-world courtesy were not what mattered to his young admirer, as an incident showed when the Prime Minister bought a paper from the young newsboy, chatted with him briefly, and was dismissed. John Diefenbaker remembered what he had said to Sir Wilfrid Laurier and not what Laurier had said to him. But it was to be many years before he occupied the same exalted office.

The tone was perhaps set during his school and college days. The sacrifices of his parents, who believed deeply in education, and particularly the determination of his mother, kept him going, though his summer earnings were disappointing, and he seldom attained the top position of which he dreamed.

He failed to secure the gold medal for oratory in his final year at Saskatoon Collegiate, though he had rehearsed for weeks. The subject was one of Laurier's favourites and on it he too should have done magnificently: "Canada's Future." Perhaps he rehearsed too much, and the speech lost spontaneity. Perhaps it sounded too good for a lad of his age, and the judges thought someone else had written it. At any rate the defeat must have been a bitter disappointment.

At college, though he was a star of the debating team, he did not become an acknowledged leader. The college paper, in a skit on students with political ambitions, saw John Diefenbaker only as leader of the opposition. Already he was running foul of the conventional, the conforming.

It is interesting to see that the first resolution he introduced in the student parliament "urged the designation of Canadian citizenship, free from the verbal trappings of racial origin".[22] Peter C. Newman in the painstakingly objective reporting of "Renegade in Power" does not comment on this, but perhaps it is worth underlining. Ardent Canadian patriotism has never seemed to John Diefenbaker to be incompatible with an emphasis on the continuity of the British tradition which has given Canada its free, democratic institutions. While he would refuse to give Pauline Johnson's Indian descent any special recognition, he would have applauded when she cried that

> "We, the men of Canada, can face the world and brag
> "That we were born in Canada, beneath the British flag."[23]

Diefenbaker was popular with his fellow-citizens in the small Saskatchewan communities in which he practised law after his war service and graduation, and was highly successful in his practice, but this was not what he wanted. From the first he was a politician. He drifted for a time into the Liberal party in a more or less informal way, but all his instincts were Conservative. He was old enough to remember the 1911 election which Laurier lost on the exciting Tory slogan "No truck or trade with the Yankees," and he must have been in sympathy with it. Certainly when he accepted the Conservative nomination for the federal seat of Prince Albert in 1925 he included "a Conservative tariff policy"[24] in his campaign. It was never popular in the West and he was defeated.

He was defeated again in 1926, this time by Mackenzie King, a politician of unparalleled skill. He was defeated in a provincial by-election in Arm River in 1928 and in the general provincial election of 1929. He was defeated in the Prince Albert mayoralty election of 1933. After the brief Anderson Conservative government was wiped out, Diefenbaker became provincial leader of his party, but again in 1938 he was himself defeated in Arm River and the Liberals "swept the province."

Then, through a rather odd series of events, almost as if it were fated, he became the federal candidate for Lake Centre and in 1940 he won his first victory. He was only forty-five, an age at which many candidates are for the first time in a position to run for such a time-consuming and costly post, but he was already a seasoned campaigner, bearing the scars of battle. He made himself felt immediately.

We were in the midst of a bitter war, and he urged a "ceasefire between political parties" for its duration. Yet he did not let his zeal for the prosecution of the war overwhelm his sense of fairness to all. He thundered against "the injustices inflicted on the Japanese Canadians"[25] (many of them born in this country and some unable to speak a word of Japanese). He pointed out that they were forced from their west coast homes, at heartbreaking material cost and under circumstances of painful and humiliating rejection which they had done nothing to deserve. It seemed strange to many that a politician willing to surrender party advantage for the sake of winning a war could at the same time utterly reject injustice to individuals as a possible measure of expediency to help win it.

Mr. Diefenbaker's career has been full of such apparent inconsistencies, but they are inconsistencies only to those who do not understand the forces motivating him. His desire for a Bill of Rights and his opposition to outlawing the Communist party sprang from the same reverence for freedom of thought, and hatred of discrimination. Like Abraham Lincoln, whom, in some outward circumstances, as in his inward strength and hearty sense of humour, he somewhat resembles, he is at heart a backwoodsman. He has always been a champion of the little man. He actually brought the entire Conservative party around to supporting the Family Allowance Act. He even dared to suggest that jail terms replace fines for business executives convicted of combining to restrain trade. And yet, while he was thus talking and acting like "the worst sort of agrarian progressive" in domestic affairs, in his loyalty to the British connection, to the royal family, to the flag, and to everything which had held Canada together during the difficult formative years, he was in the finest tradition of Canadian Conservatism.

Mr. Diefenbaker's Northern Vision was an appropriate modern successor to Sir John A. Macdonald's National Policy, but Sir John had been a politician and Mr. Diefenbaker is an idealist. Sir John was supple; Mr. Diefenbaker has always hewed to the line and let the chips fall where they would. This recalcitrance has made life harder for him, and he has sometimes reacted with bitterness and defiance, when a lesser man would have yielded.

Until 1956, Diefenbaker was more or less of a lone wolf in parliament. It is pretty well agreed that the Bay Street money was against him. The Old Guard in the Tory party feared and suspected him. The Liberals hated him. He was defeated in his attempt to win the leadership of his party in 1942, and again in 1948. Even the House Leadership of his party was denied him in those years when its titular leaders were still wandering in the wilderness trying to get into the House. In 1948 and 1952, the Liberals tried to get rid of him by gerrymandering his riding. As I was writing this I heard on the radio that there is now talk of abolishing Lake Centre altogether.

Meanwhile, within the party the mild academic agrarianism of John Bracken and the elegant, journalistic rhetoric of George Drew had alike failed to defeat the Liberals, with their entrenched power and vast financial resources. In 1956, as a measure of desperation, the disorganized and discouraged Tories turned at last to John Diefenbaker. John Diefenbaker, the country lawyer, the plain man from the prairies, the convinced and consistent Canadian, who offered his leadership-hungry fellow-countrymen, not a new flag or a creeping republicanism, but a pride in our great traditions, an exultation in our present freedom and brotherhood, and a vision of a great future.

He was chosen leader of the Conservative party in 1956, revivified and inspired the failing remnants, and scraped through to a surprising victory in 1957. It was not decisive enough to give him full control of the House, but he had tasted blood. When members proved recalcitrant, he asked for a dissolution. In 1958 he achieved an unprecedented victory, winning eight provinces including Quebec, which had not returned a Conservative majority since the days of Sir John A. Macdonald.

What happened in the next five or six years is hard to understand. He alienated his cabinet. He outraged the back-room powers that had so long governed the party and that had objected so repeatedly to his leadership. A man of stiff principles, he was uneasy in the grey areas of diplomatic compromise. Say, if you like, that this man of unquestioned probity, of dauntless courage, of deep and steadfast patriotism, came to us too late, after we had become, to all intents and purposes, a subservient satellite of the United States. Or say, with equal truth and equal inadequacy, that he came to us too early, before our young men and our young women had rejected materialism, as many of them are now beginning to do, and demanded a return to honesty, honour and mutual respect.

24

These are qualities which cannot be counterfeited, especially in a close-knit community like a small town on the prairies. To do them justice the Liberals of that day didn't even try to meet Mr. Diefenbaker on these grounds. "Better red than dead," said Mr. Pearson, with uninspiring practicality. "Who's to stop us?" blustered C. D. Howe, with American confidence. John Diefenbaker managed to stop the Liberals, for the time at least, but too many of his professed supporters were actually in agreement with them. He was still a lone wolf. He suffered under his sense of it, and his work suffered.

There was some tremendously good work done during those six years, and there were some most egregious blunders. Worse than any blunder, however, was the slow deterioration in public relations. The information media in Canada can now make or break any public figure. At a time when the financial success of a newspaper or broadcasting station depends on advertising and advertising depends on readership or viewership, such power is dangerous. Since nothing seems to attract the reader or viewer like drama, particularly scandalous or tragic drama, headlines and commentators sometimes distort the facts. Any story can be slanted, and most inevitably are. The prime minister had never really enjoyed the confidence of his own party, and when he lost the acceptance of the media he was doomed. The election of 1963 was lost before it was even called.

This is neither a political analysis nor a biographical sketch. I have not even gone through Hansard for the Diefenbaker years, much less the newspaper reports of his outside speeches, his trips and activities. In addition to the Van Dusen and Newman books which I have quoted and which are in my own library, there is plenty of material, published and unpublished, to lend credibility to a dozen different interpretations of Mr. Diefenbaker's political career and achievements. I am interested primarily in the source of strength in the man himself. What enabled him, at sixty-eight, to survive the debacle of his party, and to return to the House of Commons with his fire and dignity unimpaired? What enabled him to withstand the heartbreaking defection of his own party and their final insulting repudiation of him in 1966 and 1967, meanwhile leading them creditably through yet another election in 1965? At seventy-two, after a smashing defeat at the 1967 leadership convention in Maple Leaf Gardens, Toronto, how was he able to give his best wishes for success to the party who had so betrayed him and to the new leader? What makes him still, at seventy-eight, the lion of the House of Commons and, to many, the prototype Canadian?

He is not the man to find a second youth in a second career. His purpose is too fixed, his conviction too single-minded, his faith in himself and his country too unshakable. He will continue until the years or the wolves overtake him. Diefenbaker the Indomitable!

The High Heart—Eastern, 1943

This is the autumn heat that lies on the land,
Heavy with mist, bitter with bonfire smoke,
A harvest-sheaf bursting its braided band.
What brazen sunshine flares upon my oak
And with what fires my maple flouts the cold,
Cheapening the glitter of tulip and daffodil
Or thriftless poppies that were red and gold
When summer was a grab-bag yet to spill.
Now purple asters and the plumy shapes
Of golden-rod abound, and on the bough
Hang autumn apples and dark-clustered grapes.
The field is waiting for the winter plough,
And as the bonfires blaze against the sky
The heart of man declares life shall not die.

The High Heart—Western, 1973

New farming methods have made out-of-date
Bonfires that scarred the prairie evening skies,
But I am sure that crocuses still rise
In woolly hoods, to ask why spring is late;
For spring is still too late or early here,
Summer too hot or cold or wet or dry,
But never normal; hailstone bullets fly;
Insects and infestations still appear.
We have seen our fertile fields turn into dust
Blown with the tumbleweed across the plain,
But we still look with pride on miles of grain
And stay, since something in us says we must.
We are the soil-tamers, the pioneers,
Who sow the seed of all man's future years.

The Happy Warrior   3

The City-Dweller

This is my garden, these my forest spires;
The moon comes here, and sunset's sudden fires;
    The granite-canyoned street
    Is terrible and sweet
And full of song below the singing wires.

      Suddenly, orange flowers in the gloom,
      On slender iron stalks the street-lamps bloom;
        Their corollas of light
        Float on the misty night
      Outside the windows of my tiny room.

The organ-grinder splits the sweet spring air
With harsh and sobbing melodies, that tear
    The heart, as never note
    From lark's or robin's throat,
Stabbing in wistfulness too sharp to bear.

      My skyscraper is taller than a tree
      And bears more strange and lovely fruit for me
        The people sway and pass
        Below, like waving grass, —
      Ants in a hill whose name is history.

We are not certain where the stream will go;
We may divert the momentary flow
    Or drop one grain of sand
    Towards the promised land;
The hill will prosper and the city grow.

Nathan Phillips, Q.C.

"The Mayor of all the People", as Nathan Phillips was called in Toronto from the time of his first term, never came near to realizing his first ambition, which, like John Diefenbaker's, was to be prime minister of Canada. But his native obstinacy, of which he had a goodly share, was tempered with realism and good humour, and in the end he may have done more for his native land than if he had made it to the House of Commons or even the Provincial Legislature, for which he also tried as a second choice.

There are two lines I remember from a long poem in one of my school readers:

> "This is the happy warrior; this is he
> That every man-at-arms must wish to be."

I can remember nothing else of the poem, except that a moral odour of some sort clung about it like moth-balls, wholesome but not enthralling. It is certainly not for any moral reasons, however, that I have always associated the phrase with Nate Phillips, in spite of the probity of his life and his devotion to his job. It is because he always seemed to me to be happy in the mayoralty, not merely satisfied with his accomplishments there. His charming wife Esther (Ett) has been his constant companion. Everyone has always seemed to like and trust him. And when he came up against a stone wall it always seemed to me that he knew better than to batter his head against it. If he couldn't get over it or undermine it, he tried to get around it and attack it from another angle.

When I first joined the Metropolitan Toronto Council at the beginning of 1961, Mayor Phillips had already been a member for six years. He seemed to me to be a little weary of it all. When I had been a member for six years I could understand this, but at the time it seemed completely incomprehensible.

My good friend Marie Curtis, the reeve of Long Branch, told me that he had never forgiven Jean Newman for voting "with the suburbs" on the question of a preferred rate to the city for its water. Not to forgive so nice a woman seemed to me impossible, especially when I believed, as a suburbanite, that all the arguments were on her side. Also Mayor Phillips was an ardent amalgamationist, as indeed he remained to the end. I do not recall his speaking on any other subject than these two, though of course he must have done so.

For the most part he lay back in his chair, often with his eyes closed—the television lights were headache-making in the old York County building on Adelaide West—and only leaned forward when his attention was caught. Sometimes he even had to ask his neighbour what item had been reached on the agenda.

His weekly radio talks did nothing to change my first impression of him as a kind, bumbling old gentleman who couldn't pronounce Russian names, and spent most of his energy plying a knife and fork on the banquet circuit. I had not been long enough on the banquet circuit myself to realise what heroism it required. I was amazed later to learn that Nate had not gained a pound in the process, while I piled on forty very rapidly. I did have an inkling of the truth when Ron Haggert did a column quoting from one of Nate's radio broadcasts about a ramble through the city. Ron obviously considered it mere twaddle, and was poking fun at the mayor. The public didn't see this. There was quite a spate of correspondence thanking Mr. Haggert for putting these beautiful thoughts in permanent form for the education and delight of the public. I asked myself whether perhaps Mayor Phillips knew more about the public than Mr. Haggert did.

But the real revelation came at a provincial conference. Municipal people were talking about school costs, about which most of them didn't know much, and I, who had been a trustee for ten years, was seething. Mayor Phillips was sitting beside me in his usual relaxed pose. He rose to his feet in one lithe movement, was at the microphone, and made one of the best short speeches I have ever heard in such a discussion. He proposed a neat compromise solution, supported it with flawless logic, and was voted down almost before he had reached his seat. If he didn't shrug physically, he certainly did spiritually. He closed his eyes once more and didn't speak during the rest of the debate. But I knew then that behind that folksy, fork-wielding facade was one of the sharpest minds I'd encountered.

When I came to read Mayor Phillip's autobiography I had my eyes opened yet again. Until I got into public life myself, which I did almost accidentally, I had had very little interest in municipal affairs. I had had no idea of the disappointments which Mayor Phillips had suffered before he was finally successful, the number of strikes he had against him before he could even get started.

His family was not rich and his father was no business man. He was too small and frail as a boy to be a successful player of hockey or lacrosse. He was earning and saving from the time he was ten or twelve years old. He didn't have a Bar-Mitzvah celebration because there were so few Jews in Cornwall, where he spent his childhood. At one time he thought of dropping out of High School, because he doubted if he could get to university and fulfil his ambition to be a lawyer and enter politics. But his mother encouraged him; she was always urging him to hold his head up and aim high, and telling him tales of Ezekiel Hart and Benjamin Disraeli. And when he passed his junior matriculation he had "six or seven hundred dollars saved up"[26] and was sure he could, as he said, "double that during the two years I was articling as a student-at-law."[26] He began at three dollars a week.

Whether or not the fact that Mayor Phillips was a Jew was a strike against him I don't know, but from reading his autobiography I'm pretty sure he thought it was one. He points out that Disraeli, who was a hero to his family, would "never have been Prime Minister of England if his father had not quarrelled with the Synagogue and baptized his children. The fact is that the Jews in Canada were given the right to sit in the Parliament of Lower Canada in 1832, twenty-six years before the same right was accorded Jews in the British Parliament."[27] All of Mayor Phillips's family were loyal to their faith, and his maternal grandmother cherished a little bag of earth, reputedly from Eretz Yisroyal, which she wanted to have buried with her. If, as I suspect, he felt his path to political success was more difficult in Tory Orange Toronto, perhaps it helped to develop in him the tolerance for other ethnic and religious minorities that made him really the mayor of all the people, and dear to every one of them.

Phillips was a successful lawyer before he became a member of council. He became a King's Counsel in 1929, when he was thirty-six. In those days the Attorney General apparently restricted such appointments to lawyers who had been practicing for fifteen or more years, and since he appeared on the first list after he had been at the Bar for fifteen years and had been the youngest member of his graduating class at Osgoode Hall, the Toronto newspapers reported that he was the youngest K.C. in the province.

A hint of his approach to life is given in his autobiography when he says: "The greatest satisfaction a lawyer can get in his profession,

I feel, is to win a decision which shatters a long-standing injustice."[28]
It is interesting that he, a member of a minority group, achieved this
triumph in defence of women, who for years were perhaps the
largest under-privileged group in the world. A precedent often cited
from the Ontario Court of Appeal for half a century did not allow
a woman to sue another woman for alienation of her husband's
affections, although a man could sue another man for alienating his
wife's. To the humble but ambitious Jewish lawyer, the breaking of
this precedent was the high point in his legal career.

Nathan Phillips did not become the youngest K.C. in the province
until 1929, but he became the youngest member of the Toronto
Municipal Council in 1924. Municipal life in itself did not particularly
attract him. He saw it as a step to nomination and eventual election
in a provincial or federal riding. Little did he realize, as he says,
when he made his first election speech in Brown School that he would
be "making speeches in the same room as a candidate for the same
office for twenty-seven years."[29]

Throughout his political career he showed an aptitude for raising
popular issues which did not endear him to his fellow members of
council. Many of his suggestions were reasonable, and a few of them
were actually implemented, but their main purpose seems to have been
to keep his name before the public so that he might be considered
for a provincial or federal nomination. He did, in fact, run once
federally and twice provincially during these years, but always at
times and in places where his defeat was almost a foregone conclu-
sion. But he always came up smiling, and "tried to be philosophical
about them."[30] This training was to stand him in good stead during
the frustrations and defeats of mayoral life, in which your hottest
attacks come from those nearest you on whom you should be able
to depend for support and help.

In 1951 Alderman Phillips decided that he had been static long
enough. Things hadn't worked out according to his hopes either
provincially or federally. He would try for the mayoralty. He did
and was defeated in the campaigns for 1952 and 1953. His friends
told him to abandon the idea. He was sixty-one and out of office.
The future lay behind him. But he had faith.

In the midsummer of 1954 the entire situation changed almost
over night. Mayor Lamport, seeing that his popularity had declined,
accepted a post in the Toronto Transportation Commission. The
senior controller, Leslie Saunders, a man some six or eight years

younger than Mr. Phillips, was appointed almost automatically. He was an able man but at that time (he has since mellowed) almost bigotedly anti-Catholic and of course anti-Jewish. He was at this time Deputy Grand Master of the Grand Orange Lodge of America, and on "the glorious Twelfth", a fortnight after his elevation to the mayoral chair, he delivered a stirring speech of the sort that has kept Ireland in turmoil since 1688.

Saunders was the antithesis of Phillips who liked almost everybody and certainly wanted to keep on friendly terms with all. Phillips had been tolerant enough to move that the Council of the City of Toronto open its meetings with the "very fine" prayer called the "Lord's prayer." If he added that it "was composed for and addressed to the God of Israel by a rabbi in Israel, the founder of the Christian faith,"[31] he spoke no more than the truth, and perhaps both groups should think about the fact more often.

Members of the staff of the Toronto *Star* urged Mr. Phillips to run against Mayor Saunders and announced his candidacy. *The Telegram* followed with a supporting editorial on July 21st. The die was cast. In his sixty-second year, when most men would have been thinking of a "well-earned retirement", Nathan Phillips was preparing to embark on the eight most arduous (and consequently the most satisfying) years of his life.

Mr. Saunders, by the way, had also a high survival value. After another defeat in Toronto, he transferred his activities to East York. There, with a two-year interlude after an unsuccessful try for the top office, he has been a respected member of council for twelve years and is still sitting. Four members of the East York Council are now retired men, but they are all indefatigable workers, and very happy in their jobs, though none of the others possesses the complete self-confidence and rigorous conscience of Leslie Saunders.

No-one could make East York intolerant—it is the most open-hearted and open-handed community I know—but Toronto had certainly given pretty convincing proof of some religious and racial bias prior to Mr. Phillips's victory at the polls. He seems to have loosened the key log that broke the jam. We have had another Jewish mayor in Toronto since then, and a Catholic and a Jewish chairman of the Metropolitan Council.

It isn't necessary here to trace Nathan Phillips' career as mayor of Toronto. He has included what he considers the high lights in his autobiography. His travels and his hospitality put Toronto on the world map, and his geniality did much to destroy the old picture of the city as "Hogtown."

The picture of his character, however, would not be complete without pointing out the quiet tenacity with which he clung to his dream of a new city hall. This magnificent and unusual building was under discussion during his whole eight years in office, and he was only able to deposit a capsule of coins and historical records in the foundation of the building on November 7th of his last year in office.

The first plebiscite on the undertaking failed; the second, with the backing of Metro, better financial planning and an international architectural competition, was successful. There were problems with the judging, the tenders, the Municipal Board: all the delays which must have been so frustrating to a man who was moving ever closer to his allotted time of three-score years and ten. But he was right when he said in November, 1962: "This magnificent project of the faith of our people will spark redevelopment in a manner and to an extent which today is difficult to conceive."[32]

Not many prophets have lived to see their forecasts so amply justified.

Although Mr. Phillips has not run again for mayor since he was seventy, he and his delightful wife are still on the banquet circuit. They were at the opening of True Davidson Acres, the new Metropolitan Toronto Nursing Home in East York in June, 1973, graciously interested in all the patients, including Mrs. Isabel Ross, a former member of the Toronto Board of Education. A few days later I saw them at the civic luncheon for the Queen; they came in late for they had remained in the City Hall with the present Toronto Council to meet Her Majesty again in the square that is named after the former Mayor.

Several years ago Mr. Phillips was asked to lend his prestige and political wisdom to the Metropolitan Safety Council, of which he is still the chairman. He is interested in the Canadian National Exhibition Association, of which he is still an honorary member, and he serves on several boards of directors. At eighty-two he seems to me to be little changed, as active as ever, but not quite so pushed. He still likes people and wants them to like him, and so he goes where they are. As Lady Eaton said in her introduction to his autobiography. He "is one of those who have set the landmarks of Toronto's history."[33] She speaks of his length of service, his dream of Toronto as a convention city, his unprecedented pride in Toronto, and of course, above all, of his successful campaign for the new City Hall. But I think of his folksiness, the time he was willing to spend with little people, and his broad tolerance, and I am convinced that the feature he likes best about Nathan Phillips Square is not that it bears his name, or gives a suitable setting for his new city hall, but that day and night it is full of people. His people. All the people.

The Common Man

Happy the man who, eyeing Everest,
Finds that the pass is blocked, but pushes through
Another long and tiresome way to find
Himself upon the peak of Makalu.

Thrice happy he, if leadership of men
Has been his great achievement, if he can
Conceal the power, conceal the will, and seem
The apotheosis of the common man.

The Gentle
Heroine
4

A Woman Speaks

I am a person.
Emily Murphy and Nellie McClung and Irene Parlby proved it in the
        year of the stock market crash —
That was the men's doing! —
They proved it with Louise McKinney and Henrietta Muir Edwards
        before the judicial committee of the Privy Council,
Because the men had been too inept to find a way of settling our own
        differences at home. —
Lucky for us, as they had steadfastly turned us down in Canada. —
But not one of those five magnificent women was ever appointed
        to the Senate.
Men don't like being proved wrong,
Especially by women.
Cairine Wilson was appointed,
An ardent Liberal and a wealthy woman, perhaps a generous woman
        also, and the daughter of a Liberal senator,
A nice woman, with eight children, a womanly woman.

Twenty-five years later when a public opinion poll showed that a
        majority of Canadians wanted Agnes Macphail to be sent
        to the Senate,
When the women of Canada were demanding it , pleading for it,
Agnes who had been so brave, so good, who had done so much for
        the old, the handicapped, the delinquent,
Agnes who needed it,
Mr. St. Laurent couldn't quite bring himself to do it.

After all she had been a CCFer,
And she wasn't a womanly woman either,
Not by his standards.
She didn't know her place.

What is the place of a woman?

A woman lives to love and suffer and understand,
To suffer pain and injustice without making men uncomfortable,
To understand the needs of her country and community and people
And put them above her own desires and needs.

It is a woman's place to be slapped down again and again for
            presenting the needs of people to those who could help,
And to present them again in another way,
And again,
Firmly, gently, without arrogance or bitterness,
Until at last the needs are recognized everywhere
And some man is praised for the brilliant discovery.

Thérèse-F. Casgrain

Thérèse Casgrain! What epithet shall I attach to her name? I cannot call her Doctor Casgrain, although in 1968 she received an honorary doctorate from the Université de Montréal. I cannot call her Senator for she graced that chamber, unworthy of her as it was, for too short a time. I cannot identify her through her membership in the Order of the British Empire, conferred on her in recognition of her service on the Wartime Prices and Trade Board during the second world war, although her services here and in the consumer movement generally have been as outstanding as her services in other fields. That is the difficulty. There have been so many other fields, and in all of them her contribution has been so outstanding.

I could describe Thérèse by adding to the title of this chapter the words "née Forget", for her family background helps to explain her character and accomplishments, but she is much more than the product of that background. Perhaps her medal for distinguished service of the Order of Canada comes closer; I have never known a proud and patriotic French-speaking Canadian, of long ancestry, however bilingual, to be as sensitively aware of the problems of all Canadians and as devotedly attached to the whole Canada.

Perhaps the National Council of Jewish Women hit the mark at the time of Expo 67 when they presented her with a medal as "femme du siècle", woman of the century. This carries no title with it, and allows me to place no initials after her name. Perhaps, after all, she doesn't need them.

Both her paternal and her maternal ancestors came to Canada about the middle of the seventeenth century, less than half a century after Québec was founded by Champlain, and about the time of his death. The first Forget married the daughter of Abraham Martin, "the Scot" of the Plains of Abraham. A romantic marriage following the troubles of 1837-38 brought Scottish blood into the family again. James MacDonald, like the German Schiltzes in "Trente Arpents" so thoroughly assimilated that their name became Six, adopted French as his native tongue; his granddaughter, Blanche, became bilingual only after spending several years at an English boarding-school in Halifax.

The Forgets seem to have belonged always to the upper professional class, with strong affinities for politics and finance. Thérèse

Forget's paternal grandfather was a lawyer. Her grandmother's half-brother was the Honourable L.-O. Taillon, prime minister of Québec in 1887, again from 1892 to 1895, and later briefly, federal post-master-general. Another great-uncle, a senator, was head of the brokerage house of L.-J. Forget et Compagnie, "la plus importante maison de courtage à Montréal. . . . bien connue à travers tout le pays, et même à l'étranger."[34] Rodolphe Forget, father of Thérèse, became a partner in this firm at the age of twenty-six. There he carried out a number of daring and brilliant financial coups, "Saturday Night" writing of him on 26th November, 1910, "What Forget will cheerfully undertake in the stock market would make the average broker aghast." He became a member of parliament for the riding of Charlevoix in 1904, and was re-elected in 1908 and 1911, following which he was made "Chevalier de l'Ordre de Saint-Michel et de Saint-Georges de L'Empire Britannique."

Thérèse Forget grew up in a family which took for granted a governess and subsequent boarding-school education, a pony-cart, velvet evening dresses and pearls, a sixteen-bedroom summer home at Saint-Irénée, a few miles from the Manoir Richelieu, visits to Paris, and numerous servants. But Sir Rodolphe Forget was apparently a philanthropist with many progressive ideas for his community. He built a model farm, where stud animals were available without charge. He built hotels to encourage tourism and to provide additional justification for the railway extensions which would bring farmers nearer to their markets in cities and factories. He established a convent school at Saint-Irénée, "pourvu de bains, de lumière électrique, etc.", wherein instruction was "absolument gratuite, non seulement pour les externes, mais même pour les pensionnaires" including board, tuition and books. He paid all the expenses for more than ten years until political differences compelled him to close it. "Sir Rodolphe Forget . . . a payé chaque année tous les frais . . . à plus de $3,000 per année."[35] He offered $100,000 to a hospital campaign if the public subscription could be brought up to $150,000. La Patrie wrote of him on 18th June 1918:

> "Il est l'ami des pauvres et des affligés, des vieillards et des infirmes. Pour leur bien-être, pour apaiser leur douleur, il donne sans compter. Dans Charlevoix comme à Montréal, nombreuses sont les bonnes œuvres qu'il a encouragées et soutenues. Et tout ce bien, il le fait modestement, sans bruit,

comme s'il accomplissait les choses les plus simples du monde."[36]

The same qualities of modesty and self-control were instilled into his family from the beginning. As a small child, sitting on her great-uncle's knee while he discussed social and economic problems with her father, Thérèse found herself irresistibly tempted to braid his long white beard, and was promptly sent from the room, but when she was rude to a servant whom she disliked a public apology before the entire household was exacted. In her autobiography she speaks of it as a lesson in respecting even those we dislike, but I think perhaps it was a lesson in courtesy and consideration for all, even those least able to command it. The pleasant relations between the Forgets and their staff are witnessed by many references to later contacts.

The self-control learned so young demanded kindness to all sufferers. A blind deaf-mute, who had been caged by her parents like a little animal, was placed in charge of the nuns who managed to teach her enough that she could make her first communion. Thérèse served as her godmother. It was a harrowing experience for a young girl, but it was from such experiences that Thérèse Forget developed the deep compassion which followed her through life. Already she questioned conventional charities. The Christmas baskets and other kindnesses of the ladies of her mother's day made Thérèse ask herself why they never sought out the causes of the poverty and misery they tried to relieve.

After graduating from Sacred Heart, Thérèse continued her study of music, languages and home management, but not for long. At the annual oyster supper to raise funds for the Deaf and Dumb Institute, where she served with the other débutantes of the year, she encountered Pierre Casgrain, a young lawyer. She had met him first when she was still a school-girl, and he had then shown no special interest in her, perhaps naturally since he was then busy with his law studies. At any rate his courtship seems now to have been rapid and exciting, though strictly chaperoned, as was the custom then. They were married in January, 1916, and honeymooned in Cuba. There the young bride, with a thoughtfulness not common in her age and social group, again pondered on the extreme contrasts of riches and poverty side by side, and wondered what would come of such injustice.

The conscription issue was now dividing the country. It was clear that Sir Rodolphe Forget could no longer support the Conservative government which felt conscription was necessary. Although he had been honorary Lieutenant-Colonel of the 65th Regiment, he could not support compulsory services. He decided to retire, and his son-in-law, with whom he had many common beliefs, sought the Liberal nomination. Before she had celebrated her second wedding anniversary, Thérèse Casgrain was accompanying her husband on his campaign around the riding her father had held for so many years. The weather was frightful, so much so that on one crossing from Baie-Saint-Paul to Ile-aux-Coudres she had to be tied in the boat, but the delicately-bred, cherished young girl never flinched. Her mother had accompanied her father on such trips and she could do the same by her husband.

In Thérèse Casgrain was somehow distilled the courage and initiative of all the pioneer Frenchwomen, who, without losing their gaiety and charm, faced unflinchingly the hardships of their new homes. Perhaps she had some time to think of them during the difficult Odyssey (as she calls it) of 1917, and to wonder why all the Québecoises of today were not similarly full partners of their husbands. Those pioneer women had defended their husbands' seigneuries and homes when the men were called to Montréal or Québec on matters of larger moment. They had conducted not only their own households but the agricultural work, family industries and handicrafts which would normally be under male supervision, while their husbands sought fortunes in the fur-trade and later in the lumber industry.

> "Ces industries primitives," says Madame Casgrain in her autobiography, quoting Léon Gérin, "exercées sur de vastes espaces, à de grandes distances des établissements agricoles, ont tenu les chefs de familles, dans les paroisses nouvelles, éloignés pendant de longues périodes de leurs foyers. La mère de famille s'est trouvée pendant tout ce temps chargée de la direction non seulement du ménage, mais aussi de l'exploitation agricole. Elle a vu dès lors son influence grandir."[37]

Furthermore, the women in Québec had been the first in the British Empire to enjoy the franchise. In 1791, after the American Revolution, when the provinces of Lower and Upper Canada were created with elected assemblies, the right to vote was given to all persons with certain property qualifications. Never questioning that they were persons, the Québecoises voted until 1843 when the parliament of the new United Provinces changed the law. But wars make people think. Now in 1917, women were pouring into war industry, selling and buying victory bonds, and generally taking the place of men. They were beginning to demand the vote. It was a struggle to which the young Canadienne would soon be deeply committed, because it seemed to her a struggle for justice.

But it was not in this fight that Thérèse Casgrain made her first political speech. Although the Montreal Suffrage Association had been founded in 1913, it was made up largely of English-speaking women, and when the vote was given federally in 1918, it was disbanded in the hope that a new bilingual organization could be set up.

A second federal election confronted Pierre Casgrain in 1921, and in this the young wife again became absorbed.

Things looked harder than in 1917. Casgrain was now running against the postmaster general in the Meighen government. To make matters worse, just before the first big rally he became seriously ill with pleurisy. In response to his wife's telephone call, Ernest Lapointe came down from Québec to the rally which attracted more than a thousand people. However, he craftily induced the young wife to herself offer her husband's excuses. Women were going to vote in this election for the first time, but it was certainly not expected that they would play any other part other than a decorative or perhaps sandwich-making part in the actual election process. But this young woman's love for her husband, she tells us, gave her courage; we know she had charm, and she had listened to discussions of politics in her father's home since early childhood. She tells us something of her speech in her autobiography:

> "La rumeur courant dans le comté que mon mari se cachait par crainte de son adversaire, je leur dis: 'C'est vrai que mon mari est malade et il vous envoie, pour vous offrir ses excuses, ce qu'il a de plus cher au monde après son comté, sa femme. Il compte sur votre appui dans l'élection en cours'."[38]

M. Casgrain was again victorious, and his lovely young wife doubtless attended the first sitting of the new House. When Rodolphe Lemieux was chosen speaker, did she see foreshadowed the day when her husband would assume that honour? And did she, being what she was, notice with interest and pride that very odd figure in the worn dark-blue serge dress "far down on the left side, beyond the Conservatives, in the front row of the Progressives"? It was Agnes Campbell Macphail, the first woman to sit in the House of Commons.

In the course of the next three decades these two women, so different in background and temperament yet with such a basic community of interests, came to have a sincere respect for each other and even a mutual affection.

Mme. Casgrain speaks of Miss Macphail as "personne extrêmement éloquente que tous les députés en chambre écoutaient religieusement . . . . . .

> "Nous partagions les mêmes intérêts pour les problèmes sociaux, entre autres celui de conditions de vie de nos prisonniers, et de solides liens d'amitié nous unissaient. Un jour, alors que mon mari était président de la Chambre des communes, je me rendis à son bureau à l'improviste pour la féliciter d'un discours qu'elle venait de prononcer. A ma grande surprise, je vis sur le mur mon portrait qu'elle avait découpé dans un journal. Elle m'exprima son vif intérêt pour la lutte que je dirigeais pour l'obtention du vote des femmes dans le Québec, ajoutant que mon enthousiasme me ferait sûrement réussir. 'J'espère que vous conserverez toujours cette qualité dans les difficultés de la vie'."[39]

Miss Macphail's biographers[40] also refer to the relationship. They mention Mme. Casgrain's kindness to the slightly older woman and, the delicacy with which, when she and Mr. Speaker entertained at dinner, she would provide a suitable extra man so that Miss Macphail could be comfortably included. In spite of the country schoolteacher's admiration for the daughter of aristocratic ancestry, wealth and distinguished connections, a certain streak of Scottish "orneriness" sometimes led Miss Macphail to actions which constituted a curious form of one-upmanship. She told of once being invited to the Casgrain residence for lunch at a suggested hour "or thereabouts," which she rather stretched by arriving so late as to embarrass everyone and extremely annoy her host. It was of a piece with her wearing her old serge dress without a hat to the opening of parliament—a sort of defiance of the conventions, which, however, Madame Casgrain never seemed to hold against her.

According to her biographers, Agnes thought "naively it was a wonderful thing that a woman of rank and privilege should join the people's cause"[41] as Thérèse eventually did.

> "In Cobalt, Ontario, when Thérèse Casgrain. National Vice-President of the C.C.F., was guest speaker at a women's conference . . . Agnes, having been asked to introduce her, insisted on coming to perform this office, despite her illness. She was scarcely able to complete her introduction for her voice thickened with tears."[42]

Both Agnes Macphail and Thérèse Casgrain were strong in moral purpose with a passion for justice. Both had great personal charm and were much loved. Both achieved greatly, Agnes with a brusqueness and inpatience which made some call her mannish; Thérèse with a gentleness that disarmed anger. If Agnes was angry she didn't care whose feelings she hurt; Thérèse never wanted to hurt anyone's feelings which made her quiet but inflexible logic the more painful, perhaps, to a victim who found it hard to resist her.

Agnes had a raw-boned Scottish figure, and looked the picture of health, but her biographers often speak of her having worked herself into exhaustion, and record at least two operations and a stroke, which put a period to her activity. She died at the age of sixty-four, in loneliness, financial insecurity and a sort of resentment that must have made her very unhappy. Thérèse, a slender girl, looking like a frail lily in her wedding portrait, lived as tough a life as Agnes's, with as many frustrations and disappointments, yet, when I last saw her, two years after she retired from the Senate at the statutory age, she was as interested as ever in current problems and talked knowledgeably about the environment and the need for open space in urban centres.

I am not going to list the achievements of either woman. They will be found in the books to which I refer, and it is not the purpose of these sketches in any case to give balanced biographies. I am trying to find why the years seem so much kinder to some of us than to others. Why to some are the sixties and seventies and even the eighties, times of ripeness and harvest and, eventually, of "quiet coves" where life "furls its wings"

> ". . . contented so to look
> On mists in idleness—to let fair things
> Pass by unheeded as a threshold brook."[43]

43

Why to others are they "winters of pale misfeature" or terrible and destroying storms? We should all "go down with unreluctant tread, Rose-crowned, into the darkness."[44] To do this, except in the exaltation of some youthful ecstasy of devotion and sacrifice, one must become a complete human being, willing, and indeed glad, to experience the whole of life.

There are some aspects of the life and character of Thérèse Casgrain that help to explain her high survival value.

In the first place she had no resentment of men, none of what is called masculine protest. It has been so strong in many successful women that it has made it impossible for them to marry. This has always seemed to me to be the case with Charlotte Whitton, former mayor of Ottawa, whom I greatly admire. Her activities and remarks are a constant source of delight and pride to all women, but I would never look to her for an example of a complete and well-adjusted life. Charlotte has all the fighting spirit of her Irish ancestors and the attempts of men twice her size, with half her brains and a quarter of her drive, to patronize her and talk down to her, must have established this masculine-protest to such a point that I have heard her snarl at a man who tried to open a door for her or suggested she sit down to speak because she had been in an accident. Agnes Macphail liked men and liked their admiration, but when it came to marriage

> "the basic choice was the same: *her* life, *her* work—or the wifely role as helpmate to a man?"[45]
>
> "To her, then (at fourteen) and forever after, marriage implied submission, constant catering to the whims of a man, and days too full of distasteful tasks to leave time for outside interests."[46]

Every women's liberationist should read, first, the biography of Agnes Macphail, and then the autobiography of Thérèse Casgrain. Thérèse was married at about the age at which Agnes finished high school. There was nothing in Mme Casgrain's home life to make her shrink from marriage. Her mother, whom she describes as "épouse douce et soumise, mère attentive, . . . le prototype de la jeune femme candide d'autrefois,"[47] nevertheless managed to accompany her husband on many of his trips, and was always treated by him with the utmost consideration. Even the children were drawn into great events in the family and had the opportunity to have their lives enriched by meeting and hearing the cultured and widely experienced guests who were often in the home.

This is man's world, but many men have an inferiority complex for which they over-compensate by snatching and clawing for "success", for money and status. With successful women this is even more likely to be a factor. There was nothing of it in Thérèse Forget. She did not have to struggle for money and position: she had them. Through her father and her husband alike, she had a recognized position. She was at home in any society: as good as the best, no better than the worst. Her public activity was spurred by the sort of "noblesse oblige" philosophy which characterizes the finest aristocrats. Defeat does not daunt them: they are only sorry not to have been able to make others see the road to their own well-being.

In her youth Thérèse Forget had learned self-discipline. An ideal had been placed before her. A woman. When she speaks of her mother as "douce", it is easy to translate this as sweet or gentle, but it is also defined in Bélisle's "Dictionnaire Général de la Langue Française au Canada" as "having dignity, forgiveness, humanity." "Candide" is defined as having the moral quality which enables a pure, innocent soul to show itself as it is, without fear or suspicion. And if the non-aggressive quality of the protests of the Québecoises, their tendency to obey the laws, even the unjust laws, delayed some of the reforms they sought, they won them eventually, and without destroying the essential fabric of their society.

Never afraid to say what she thought should be said, or to do what she felt had to be done, Thérèse Casgrain never, throughout a long life of heroic public activity, lost her dignity, her charm, and her essential womanliness.

She has been a devoted wife, the loving but firm mother of four children, a gracious hostess and in every way a great lady. While her husband sat in the House of Commons and her children were growing up, she felt that her home was her primary responsibility. At the same time she was not content only with the old female role of Lady Bountiful, and worked long and steadily for justice to women and particularly the women of her own province. When her husband became a judge in 1942, she had worked for twenty years for woman suffrage in Quebec without ever losing her temper or her charm, had worked to help the Japanese victims of wartime prejudice, and had organized women's groups for half Canada under the Wartime Prices and Trade Board. Shortly after Pierre Casgrain's elevation to the judiciary she spearheaded a protest against a plan to humiliate the women of Québec and affect the rights of many children by giving family allowance cheques to the husbands in this only of all provinces.

Meanwhile she had been following the history of the CCF and could not help wondering why social measures such as old-age pensions, unemployment insurance and family allowances had always to be urged first by this new and supposedly dangerous party. They seemed to be taken up by the old parties only under pressure and for opportunistic motives. She had always lived by the dictum that money should serve men, not men money. She decided to join the C.C.F.

Before doing so, however, in accordance with her character, she talked it over with her husband. He did not oppose her. Indeed on the occasion of Prime Minister King's death, he wired her at a C.C.F. convention suggesting the advisability of a message of condolence, and joined with her in a letter of regret to Bishop Charbonneau when the latter had retired from his bishopric because of Duplessis' vengeance for the Bishop's help to the Asbestos strikers. By this time, in her quiet way, Mme. Casgrain had become well known in Québec as the friend of rich and poor alike, and when a rude fellow, obviously addicted to the bottle, made a slighting remark to her during a demonstration against a new and very harsh labour code, another put him in his place with an abrupt "Toi tais-toi, et laisse la 'petite mère' du Québec tranquille!"[48]

Thérèse Casgrain never pushed herself. When she was elected vice-president of the national C.C.F., she was not even at the convention and had not given permission for her name to be put in nomination. She was similarly elected leader of the party in Quebec while she was representing the C.C.F. at an international rally of democratic socialist movements in Frankfurt, Germany, where, with the aid of the Scandinavians, she managed to secure a council seat for Canada. Eight times she ran for election, with little hope, as a woman and leader of the left-wing party, of accomplishing more than familiarizing the public with the philosophy and aims of democratic socialism.

In his introduction to her autobiography Professor Frank R. Scott points out that her struggle for the rights of women was but a part of her struggle for human rights in general, men's and children's as well as women's, for consumer rights, civil liberties and world peace, and above all for harmony and co-operation between the two great founding groups of this country. Professor Scott believes she saw these needs with a sure intuition rather than a logical analysis. But what is intuition other than the computer in the brain clicking out the answer too rapidly for its movements to be followed? If the programming has been right, the answer will be right. It has always been right with her. And once the path was clearly indicated, there has never seemed to be any conflict in her mind or heart. She has followed it with all the patient courage and feminine charm of her ancestresses.

A Flower

A woman in a world of men
Is like a flower in a fen;
But if its sweetness and its light
Are such as fens can never blight,
It may inspire us to renew
The fen; and women can make men do
Things that they always knew were needed
That trade and politics left unheeded,

There sometimes is an unsuspected power
In being uncompromisingly a flower.

The
Life Force

5

A Woman's Role

> How foolish to confine a tree
> With brick or stone, above, below!
> If it has food and drink and air
> It grows because it has to grow.
> It crumbles brick, displaces stone,
> And makes a roothold of its own.
>
> Women, I think, are like the tree,
> For if you say, "Not here! Not there!"
> The life that is impelled to grow
> Finds other outlet otherwhere.
> Stronger than nature, man or fate,
> Women must serve, conserve, create.

Miss Vida Peene, S.M.

Perhaps Shaw is right when he talks about women as the life-force. There are several women I know who seem to me to be irresistible forces looking for supposedly immovable objects to play with. Of these Vida Peene is one of the most interesting but she is also one of the hardest to write about. In fact, there has been very little written about her, though much about the causes in which she has interested herself. Her award of the Medal of Service of the Order of Canada, however, is a good guidepost to her life story.

Although Vida Peene is about my own age, she seemed much older when I first encountered her in University Women's Club work. She seemed so confident, so knowledgeable, so important, while I was still uncertain of my future and without any particular confidence in my ability to achieve anything worth while. As I have learned more about her, I realize that her problems were probably just as great as mine, though rather different.

Her mother belonged to a generation of women with a strong masculine protest. Ibsen wrote his play "A Doll's House", in 1879 but it was not published or played in England until the nineties. At the same time it was part of a wave of unrest which swept through the women of the bourgeoisie during the last quarter of the century, set in motion by complex social and economic conditions that there is no room to analyze here. A strong, aggressive woman, with talents and skills she could see no way of using, felt that she was a Nora in a Doll's House of her own, that her husband didn't understand her, that he didn't try to understand her, that no men understood women, and that marriage was somehow a diminution of herself. At the same time that she would try to push her daughters into matrimony, she would subconsciously warn them against it. I have seen this in the case of a number of my contemporaries, and only some such problem seems adequate to explain the reasons why Vida never married, in spite of her charm, intelligence and money .

Apparently she did not reject marriage because she looked forward to a career. Some years ago, when she was first appointed to the board of the O'Keefe Centre, the *Globe Magazine* published an article by Betty Lee in which Miss Peene is quoted as saying: "There was really nothing I would have been allowed to do. . . . Most girls of the time either found a husband or went into domestic service or took a teaching position. When I thought about it, I knew I didn't want to teach."

Five women had graduated from medical school in Toronto as early as 1890, and there were women lawyers too but before the first world war the average girl still thought of the professions other than teaching as the natural domain of men. Ann Fasken Baird, the mother of Margaret Campbell, was a builder and contractor, building her first house when she was eighteen, and opening forty houses on Brock Avenue north from Bloor Street a couple of months before Margaret was born. This is the sort of thing that I imagine might have interested Vida Peene, but it is unlikely that she ever heard of it, or that her mother would have thought it a suitable occupation in any case. I know my parents were appalled when my sister and I went into business as late as the twenties, and it was the publishing business, which might have been thought "nice" enough even for ministers' daughters.

Vida's father was wealthy, and her mother was interested in music and the theatre—culture was considered a suitable interest for a woman even in those limited pre-war days. According to Miss Lee's article Vida finished her high school work at thirteen and wanted to matriculate and go to college. Fortunately her parents would not allow this. However precocious mentally, no girl is ready for university at thirteen. She studied in England and Germany, came home to Hamilton before the outbreak of war in 1914, and was enrolled by her parents in an art school. She was still considered too young for university or, one presumes, a proper début, but when she was sixteen she undertook to brush up on sixteen junior matriculation subjects. She passed and later passed again in an honour course including analytical geometry, algebra, Latin and ancient history. She took her B.A. at the University of Toronto, and a two-year post-graduate course in Household Science. Then she studied interior decoration at the College of Art.

The Globe Magazine article does not say much about Vida Peene's father except that he was an architect and financier. It seems to me that she must have inherited some of the qualities that made him successful, although on the surface her mother seems to have made the greater impression. It was her mother who insisted that one did not work for money unless one needed it, but the fact remains that Vida did give lectures on interior decoration for four years and after that wrote newspaper columns for several more years under the pen-name of Susan Proctor. I have not had a chance to read these columns but they must have seemed pretty dull work to the author after the first few months.

To have no regular occupation would have been worse to a person of Vida Peene's energy. Besides she was never one to take her hand from the plough before finishing the furrow. Her record was only five short of a thousand columns in twenty years, which comes to about one a week with two weeks' holidays per year.

In addition to her long interest in the profession of decorating, which might be considered ancillary to her father's profession of architecture, Vida seems to have inherited his aptitude for commerce and finance. In addition to managing her own business affairs, which are not small, she has shown a skill in grappling with facts, preparing reports and organizing committees. Combined with a flair for recognizing the right person for every job, these qualities have made her more than a fashionable volunteer in everything she has undertaken. She finished one horrendous job for the Canadian Federation of University Women, not only well within her time limit, but also at a saving of $4,000 on the budgeted cost of the project. If only we could find people like that in politics or the civil service.

Life for her really began at forty when she put her skills to use as a commandant in the Canadian Red Cross during the Second World War. The Red Cross was making plans for handling the civilian population in case of bombing or gas attacks. Vida turned the dietetic side of things over to staff members who were professional dietitians, telling them to plan emergency meals that would be nourishing and could be prepared in large quantities, indoors or outdoors, hot or cold. She turned her own attention to corps administration, finance, and such projects as a survey of possible sites for mass accommodation if large sections of the city had to be evacuated.

She had found herself in what some would consider the dry dust of organization, but when the war was over the Red Cross was not for her. It was too routine, too repetitious. She needed ever new challenges. Naturally, as they always do when the irresistible force gets going, they presented themselves. She undertook to supervise ticket sales for the Dominion Drama Festival in 1949. After that she never looked back.

In 1962 she was president of the Dominion Drama Festival, but she had acquired many other interests on the way. She was president for two years of the Central Ontario Drama Festival, branch liaison chairman for the National Ballet Guild, active in the Canadian Opera Association, the Canadian Opera Women's Committee and the Opera Guild, and organized the Allied Arts Council. She had underwritten a survey of auditorium facilities across North America, and she had helped many struggling performers to further study. She has also helped the Toronto Arts Foundation, the University Alumnae Dramatic Club, and the Province of Ontario Council of the Arts, and has sat for years on the board of the O'Keefe Centre.

In 1967, when she might have been retired if she had been a teacher, far from slowing up, she added to her club and committee work two special projects. She compiled the centennial catalogue of two hundred Canadian three-act plays, the earliest dating back to 1606, which was used by the Dominion Drama Festival in preparing its centennial programme. And she organized and saw through the press, for the Canadian Federation of University Women, a 20-part biographical dictionary of outstanding Canadian women: none of the living were included since their careers were not complete.

Nor has she settled down since. When plans for this book were being considered I saw with surprise that she had taken on the presidency of the Women's Canadian Club. Membership has been dropping a little, and the nominating committee wanted someone with a great name, an outstanding record of success, and boundless energy, to tackle the job.

People will ask why she bothers with this when she could be "taking life easy," just "enjoying herself." She *is* enjoying herself. When Betty Lee asked her why she undertook such arduous tasks and held herself to them with such unswerving dedication, she reports that Miss Peene said it was fun. Not for power or prestige, but for fun. I believe her.

An athlete has to use his muscles. He stretches. He flexes his arms. He competes with others, using every last ounce of strength and energy. And he enjoys it. He is doing what he does best. If he gets plaudits and awards, that's jam on the bread and butter, but it's only jam after all. It isn't the essential food of the soul.

I know many women who have found happiness after retiring from a profession in pursuing an interest which has arisen out of that profession or some hobby for which there has never been enough time before. Lila Ellison, our first woman school principal in East York, is still giving leadership in her church and with a group of retired teachers. When I finished my first draft of this book, Dorothy

Hague, the former reeve of Swansea, who left politics, undefeated, many years ago, was still working on the Historic Sites Advisory Board of the Metropolitan Toronto Conservation Authority, and taking a keen interest in Black Creek Pioneer Village. I saw her at a recent meeting and she didn't look a day older than when she retired, still friendly and gracious, beautifully groomed and exquisitely dressed. She died not long before the book went to press, loved and wanted to the end. Agatha Leonard, who graduated with me from the University of Toronto, was taking tickets for the last University Alumnae play I attended; her beautiful black hair has turned gray but otherwise she doesn't look very different from the young Agatha Leonard of 1921. She has still the same enthusiasms.

Cecilia Long may have one of Dr. Wilder Penfield's "second careers" as head of the Metropolitan Toronto Zoological Society. It requires some of the same stamina, unquenchable enthusiasm, and ability to infect others with her own faith, that she must have required as a successful advertising woman. She expects to retire from her public relations job with the Arthritis and Rheumatism Association of Canada at the usual time, but will stay with the Zoo as long as she is needed. Then she will seek some new venture, for her incurable zest for life would make it impossible for her ever to sit for very long with her hands folded.

But the case of Vida Peene is different. I know of no-one else who has made a career of being both a voluntary patron and an indefatigable servant of the arts, often young arts, badly in need of both patronage and service. And I can imagine no-one else who could carry it on to the age of three score and ten and still be taking on new responsibilities.

I venture to prophesy that the Women's Canadian Club of Toronto will not know what has happened to it when it foregathers again this Fall. The dust will have been shaken out of its skirts; its financial affairs will have been straightened up; its membership rolls will be unbelievably increased, and all sorts of committees will be working like beavers. And it will all be tied in with Miss Peene's other activities, helping and being helped by them, like pieces of a jigsaw puzzle, for that's the way her organizing mind works. It's the greatest game in the world, if you can play it well. And Vida Peene plays it superlatively.

Motivation

There is a beauty in a great machine,
Precision-tooled, exact to a degree
Eye cannot recognize; edges are keen
And movement is a clanging harmony.

But there is also beauty in a man
Or woman whose co-ordinated grace
And strength of sinew and of muscle can
Superbly lift or throw or leap or race.

And there is beauty in the human mind,
Sorting the essential from the amorphous heap,
The unprogrammed, balanced judgement, undesigned
Power that wells up from the subconscious deep.

We praise all three, who see their active hour,
But do not see what activates the power.

The Bulldozer 6

Strength

The strong will find a way —
Will find their destiny,
Whatever that may be.
The weak will sway,
Falter and grope
And fall;
They have a flaccid hope
But no great faith, no loyalty at all.

> The strong will tear aside
> Garland or rope
> That tries to hold them down.
> They have an energy
> That's not ambition, pride,
> Duty, creative urge,
> But some exultant surge
> That is no more to be denied
> Than rivers that must find the sea,
> Even as the fragile drown.
> Nothing can hold them back.
> At racing speeds
> They will tear out, through weaker things, a track
> That, being torn, may spoil
> A softer, richer soil,
> And yet, harnessed, that stream
> May save man hours of toil
> And realize a dream.

Fred Gardiner: Big Daddy

Frederick G. Gardiner has a string of honours after his name so long that you could make a story out of these alone. Indeed, if trying to understand Vida Peene is difficult because there is too little information available about her, trying to understand Fred Gardiner is difficult because there is too much. While other great ones of our day have a clipping or two in the general biographical section of the Metropolitan Toronto Reference Library, or at most a single slim flat file that's hard to find in the crowded drawers, Mr. Gardiner has a file so fat that the only difficulty is getting it out. And it only goes back a few years at that.

Of course, there probably isn't a file like that on him in Vancouver or Halifax, but I don't suppose there's anyone in government or allied fields in Canada who doesn't know something of the first chairman of Metropolitan Toronto. From all over this continent, and indeed from all over the world, legislators, planners, engineers, and others have come to study the experiment which he fathered. The Metropolitan area now comprises two million people, and is still growing. Big Daddy, indeed!

At seventy-eight he is still in the lime-light. Still, as Michael Best put it recently in the Toronto *Star*, "the growling desk-banging, finger-stabbing Gardiner that used to orchestrate Metro Council like a roughhouse Toscanini." But if he was able to get a bunch of locally-minded politicians, some over-timorous and others over-aggressive, and all defensive of their own and suspicious of the other municipalities—if he was able to get this group, I say, playing together as a Toscanini orchestra, I don't think most people would worry about what tactics he used.

When I call him a bulldozer, I am not being critical. A bulldozer knocks things about a bit, but not wantonly. There is a purpose, and usually the purpose is to prepare for construction. And so it was with Big Daddy. He had to clear away the obstacles and build a region.

The thirteen municipalities of Metro Toronto had no desire to become a region. North York, and some of the smaller municipalities which had no direct contact with the lake, still had to get their water from it. There seemed no way to get the big trunk mains up to them except through Toronto. And why should Toronto inconvenience its citizens for North York? And who should pay? The papers ran a story that they were bathing the babies in ginger ale; soda water seems more likely, and it might be pleasant, though not perhaps for an infant. Anyway something had to be done. And there was a problem with roads too. The city had big plans but the suburbs wouldn't go along with them. The suburbs were strangling the city over communications, and the city was starving the suburbs for water.

The province took the initiative. The legislation was rough and ready, but it worked. And the reason it worked, most people agreed, was because of the chairman appointed by the province.

Frederick G. Gardiner, Q.C., had been deputy reeve and reeve of the little village of Forest Hill, and chairman of its hydro commission. He had been a member of the Toronto and Suburban Planning Board and the Toronto and York Planning Board. He had been warden of York County. He had also been—and this is a much more influential position than any of the above—a principal fund-raiser for the Conservative Party which seems to hold power by hereditary right in Ontario. And he had nominated Leslie Frost as leader of that party, which meant that he had nominated him for the premiership. That is, he had provided the general and the war chest.

It is said that when the late Mr. Frost offered the Metro chairmanship to Fred Gardiner, Fred growled that he hadn't spent thirty years building up a law practice, to throw it away at his age. It is also said that Frost pointed out that his old friend had not hesitated to take him away from his law practice. If it is true, both men must have been joking. They had politics in their blood, both of them, the one at the municipal and the other at the provincial level. No one with twenty years of municipal experience could have resisted the challenge to see what he could do with Metro.

Big Daddy did a lot. When he left, at the end of 1961, most of the big trunk water-mains and sewers were in, the Gardiner Expressway needed to be extended into Scarborough, but the worst was over. The Don Valley Parkway was done as far as it was needed, and on the last day of his last term—or night, I should say, for we sat until six o'clock in the morning—he got concurrence with the Spadina Expressway by telling us that the provincial government insisted on it as the price of providing an interchange for Yorkdale at Highway 401.

Personally I was very fond of Mr. Gardiner. Unlike some of the women who served on Metro Council, I was never alarmed by his voice or language or hectoring manner. I had come from the world of business, not from the protection of a home, and I had met tougher characters than Fred Gardiner in my day. Besides, in most cases I agreed with him. I did, however, object to his tactics of beating council into submission by holding the meetings until members were so exhausted by hunger and weariness that they would vote for anything. I used to move regularly for supper intermissions, but Margaret Campbell was the only one who dared to second me, and the vote never supported us. The men were all craven; after all, the Metro Chairman was the "fountain of honour" from whom emanated appointments, entertainment tickets, banquet invitations and other amenities of a political career.

When we did have a lunch or dinner break the chairman would never eat with the rest of us. At night I'm told he went for a Turkish bath and massage. At any rate he always kept his distance. On jaunts to projects he sometimes acted like a kind but authoritarian father and at other times like a hot-tempered king who is father of his country in name only. I should not be surprised if he put quite a number of people in the way of making quite a bit of money, for he favoured development, but that didn't bother me as much as some, unless the development was a bad one. It always seemed to me that he felt you couldn't make an omelette without breaking eggs. After all, the whole basis of our society is wrong. You can hardly operate and change it at the same time. Big Daddy had no desire to change society; he only wanted it to work well for him and his, and "his" included Metropolitan Toronto.

I don't know why I should talk of him in the past tense, for at seventy-eight he is still very active. After he left the Metropolitan chairmanship he served from 1963 to 1967 as vice-president of the Canadian National Exhibition Board, preparing for the Centennial, and he has now been for some years a member of the Toronto Hydro Commission. When the 1973-4 Toronto Council refused to accept the executive recommendation to reappoint him to the latter job, but insisted on receiving applications, he surprised everyone by saying it was a quite a good idea. He came along with the pipe-fitters, typesetters and other miscellaneous applicants, spoke and aswered questions for an hour, and Gardiner was appointed by an overwhelming majority. Executive Alderman Carl Jaffary, no friend to the Conservatives, said afterwards he'd learned more about Hydro in that hour than he'd learned during all the rest of his political career.

So there he is, for another two years. Will he be back at eighty?

I wouldn't put it past him. He is still a partner in the law firm of Gardiner Roberts. By his own admission, he is president of four corporations, vice-president of three more, and a director of eight others.

Two years ago he was in a wheel-chair. Then he had a three-hour operation which gave him an artificial hip-joint, a steel ball in a plastic socket. He was determined to walk again, although he once said that the chief attraction of the hydro position was the chauffered car provided to commissioners. Certainly a yearly salary of $8,000 it not enough to pay for a large portion of the time of a corporation lawyer.

But Fred Gardiner likes to be active. He seems to think a man is somehow less than a man if he's not active. He will express an opinion about politics—particularly Metro politics—at the drop of a hat, and when anything particularly striking or outrageous is done the newsmen usually ask his opinion. It is always salty, colourful and delightfully frank. He can put more meat in a sentence than most of us can in a ten-course meal. But he's not a contemplative type. If he ever tackles his own autobiography, I hope he does it with the aid of a ghost-writer, a couple of secretaries and a messenger boy.

I don't know what he would be like in defeat, for I doubt if he's ever met much of it. I don't know whether he could go through what John Diefenbaker has gone through and still kept that ardour for combat. I don't know anything about his home life either, but I don't think he's the man to settle down in old age and find satisfaction in living for his children and grandchildren. You find fulfilment or frustrations in life according to what you live for, and if you lose that at the end you have lost everything. Mr. Gardiner could be very unhappy if he had to spend his last years as an invalid, and I hope he never has to. If he does he will ride down pain with the same singleness of purpose with which he has ridden down opposition.

Prayer

> O God of strength, give me the fire to fight
> Life's battle to the end.
> Is man a brittle stalk that he should break,
> A wavering reed that he should bend?
> But, God of mercy, give me steel to bear
> Defeat, if that is what You send.

The
Traders

7

Business

Business!

Once high desks, with shirt-sleeved, dark-vested clerks scribbling
       furiously,
Sometimes seated on stools, sometimes standing,
Underpaid and overworked,
And now, in velvet jackets with long curls and beards, tending
       computers,
Underworked and overpaid, and mistakes harder to find than ever.

Salesmen dashing about with sample cases of various sizes, containing
       goods of various qualities,
Most of them cheaply attractive with built-in obsolescence,
Always trying to get good deals for good customers, and claiming
       credit for doing so whether they've done it or not,
And always grumbling about expense accounts.

Stenographers chewing their gum and filing their nails and slopping
       tea in saucers,
Coming late in the morning and leaving early at night and talking
       on the 'phone to their boy friends,
And crocheting in the john as a means of getting a second coffee break,
With their own ideas of spelling and punctuation,
And no idea at all of the English language, ni de français non plus si
       elles sont de cette langue.

Day after day.
Year after year.
And then retirement
On an inadequate pension.
Is this life ?
Is it all?

NO, it is not all.
Business can be an adventure, an education, an entertainment, an
      ever-changing challenge and interest.
It can command the ardour of a knight on his first quest, the
            dedication of Joan of Arc, the devotion of Patient Griselda,
Devotion far beyond the call of duty,
A dedication to service,
A world of romance,
A creative process fusing all energies and ideas in one white heat
      of achievement.

Business itself is not dull,
Though dull people can make it seem so.

Oakah Jones & Roy Britnell

Business is a game I have enjoyed myself in my day. It didn't have the answer for me, because I didn't find fulfillment in it; or perhaps I didn't find fulfillment in it because it didn't have the answers. It has certainly had the answers for a great many, and they have found fulfillment in it too. Two of whom I have become very fond over the years are Roy Britnell, because I have almost always shared his views and tastes, and Oakah Jones in spite of the fact that I have almost always disagreed with him.

Both of these men are keenly interested in politics, and have exercised considerable influence, but neither is a professional politician. Neither is primarily interested in the government of men and the shaping of national or even local destinies. They are interested primarily in policies which affect their own businesses and those like them, or their own social and economic class. They would both quite sincerely deny this, because they would consider the comment somehow depreciatory and I do not mean it so; I am merely establishing what seem to me to be their priorities. In a somewhat more restricted fashion they resemble the gentleman who said: "What's good for General Motors is good for the United States." He had arguments to prove it, and they have arguments for their positions. Their businesses have provided them with satisfying careers in the milieus in which they work, and although they have continued to work at them after the normal deadline, they have brought in others to replace them gradually so that the continuity of their businesses can be preserved. As Kipling puts it: "The game is more than the player of the game, And the ship is more than the crew."[49]

Oakah L. Jones was born in 1901 in Boston, Massachusetts, and attended Malden and Everett High Schools, Brown University and the University of Tulsa. In many ways he is an Oklahoman, as his name implies (I understand the L was added for euphony, or just for the 'ell of it, and doesn't stand for anything). He started work at sixteen as a clerk, and early determined his bent, which was for energy production and distribution. At eighteen he moved to the Cape Breton Electric Co., in Sydney, Nova Scotia, which handled railways and ferries among other activities. There he seems to have felt very comfortable. There is a close tie between the Maritime Provinces of Canada and the New England States, because of their geographical neighbourhood and similar natural features and economic resources. At any rate, Mr. Jones liked to it enough that in 1954, when he assumed the management of the Consumers' Gas Co., he was able to talk about coming home.

Like other ambitious young Americans, Mr. Jones, though he had determined his general field, was not anxious to tether himself to one post in it. He had short-term jobs in Connecticut and Rhode Island before moving to what looked like a permanent billet in Oklahoma. I say it looked permanent not only because it was a long move geographically but also because it was a switch from electricity to gas.

Starting as assistant secretary and treasurer of the Oklahoma Natural Gas Co. in 1935, he became vice-president in 1951 and did not leave until 1954. Meanwhile he served in all sorts of civic capacities, and seemed to have thoroughly settled in. His ability was recognized. He sat on the Advisory Council of the University of Tulsa, and was a consulting professor on management at the Oklahoma Agricultural and Mechanical College. He was president of the Tulsa Chamber of Commerce. He also served as president of the National Office Management Association, and from time to time received various honours and responsibilities.

At the age of 53 he decided to move to Canada. It was a big step for a middle-aged man, a drastic change in climate, a whole new set of acquaintances to make as well as new business contacts to establish and a completely new staff to manage, under new customs, new labour regulations and tax laws and all sorts of other strangenesses. He would have good law advice and good technical assistance, for he was coming to be vice-president and general manager of the Consumers' Gas Company, but he would be bound to encounter some problems, particularly as the company didn't have too good a public image, and was having to switch from manufactured to natural gas.

Before too long Mr. Jones became president, and finally chairman of the board. He also accumulated honours and responsibilities which more than made up for those he had abandoned in Oklahoma, and helped to change the public image of his company. Some of these were in the field of allied business such as posts in Home Oil Co., Niagara Gas Transmission Limited, Shorgas Ltd., and Boiler Inspection Insurance Company. Others were of a more general nature. Many were in the field of public service, not strictly of business at all, though business experience and acumen were desirable qualifications. It is a formidable list, but a few of the items must be recorded to measure something of the stature of the man: Member of the Board of Governors of Trinity College and of the Board of Regents of Mount Allison University, one of the Toronto Harbour Commissioners, chairman of the board of the Ontario Research Foundation, vice-president of the Metropolitan Toronto Industrial Commission, member of the Toronto Redevelopment Advisory Council, and the Ontario Economic Council, President of the Canadian National Exhibition Association, a member of the Synod of the Anglican Diocese of Toronto, and a director of the Boy Scouts Association and the Toronto Symphony Orchestra Association.

He probably couldn't himself, offhand, list all his varied connections; I'm sure he must have had frequent date conflicts, and needed a secretary to push him off to his various appointments, and yet every organization with which he has been connected has felt that it was his particular pride and joy and had the lion's share of his attention.

Mr. Jones, or Dr. Jones, as I suppose we should call him, since he has an honorary LL.D., is a strange combination. He never seems to push himself, and yet he always gets his own way. Unusually in the end everybody is satisfied. He seldom criticizes anyone, or even openly opposes them, but he is equally seldom swayed by their arguments. He likes young people and gets along with them. He is very loyal to his friends, and will put himself out greatly for them. And somehow he has a knack with finances. Every organization with which he has been closely associated has improved its financial status while he has been in charge. He's an idea man himself, and he encourages others, at the same time gently restraining them from going out on a limb and sawing it off behind themselves.

When he was president of the Canadian National Exhibition Board I saw more of him than I have before or since. There were two matters on which we were seriously at odds, and I don't think I made any headway with either.

All the men on the Canadian National Exhibition Board would be described by the women's lib group in language unsuitable for print, and yet with which I cannot but largely agree. They place women in two main classes; their own wives and the wives of men like themselves, shining in the reflected glory of their husbands and invited to special occasions which they adorn—the pretty dears with their flowered chiffons and exquisite hairdos; and devoted staff members who do the work so that some man can take the credit. The two or

64

three women members of the Board of Directors felt that "women's day" was a patronizing concession to a sex which included outstanding members in almost every field of activity stressed at the exhibition. We suggested that giving women a special day for their special little feminine interests, was putting them on a level with children, who also required special concessions and attractions. Finally, in desperation, I said, "Then why not have a men's day?" Oakah looked at me with that radiant smile, and made the retort of his C.N.E. career: "But, True," he said kindly, "every day is men's day."

My other reason for being vexed with him was that although I was on the planning committee, and attended exhibitions regularly and made copious notes, I never had a chance to try to get any of my ideas implemented. There were always planning committee meetings, but staff reports took up all the time, and if any was left over it was spent in asking questions of the experts. Oakah always insisted that there was going to be lots of opportunity to participate in the planning, but he is too intelligent not to have known that there wasn't and wouldn't be. I think he distrusted the brain-storming sessions which some executives claim are useful, and felt that the main function of a committee was to approve the recommendations of the officers or officials. It is certainly a much more efficient and rapid way to operate, and he did it so genially that you could never get as angry at him as you wanted to. You found yourself laughing in spite of yourself.

In an interview given to the *Star* in 1971, Oakah Jones, said that at seventy he was easing himself towards retirement. He was still the chairman of the board but the day-to-day administration had been turned over to the new president. Asked about the Home Oil take-over, Mr. Jones was vague and turned the Star over to one of the two executive vice-presidents who had recently been appointed, but said that no mergers were being planned. At that time he was still "chief executive officer" of Consumers' Gas, but said "I'm not operating that way."

Mr. Jones became a Canadian citizen in 1962. He said he wanted to stop feeling "inhibited about expressing himself about Canadian politics," but I would take this as more or less of a joke. In the first place he hasn't expressed himself publicly about politics any more since 1962 than he did before; that's not the way a successful business man works. In the second place he very seldom treats a question of that sort seriously. When he became a citizen I would wager it was because he thought it would help the business or because he had decided he had really become a Canadian and might as well make it legal. Probably it was a bit of both.

Roy Britnell, like Oakah Jones, is friendly and approachable and tells you very little about himself. He will spend as much time as you like telling you why Canada should adhere to the Florence agreement regarding the remission of all duty on books, musical instruments, art works, etc., giving you all the cons as well as the pros. He will talk about education, pornography or municipal transportation. In the midst of it he sometimes drops a hint of his own life and his views of his work in the world.

He started work at sixteen, although he wanted to go on to school and college and become a lawyer. His father, Albert Britnell, who had come to Canada from Oxfordshire, England, in 1893, and started a little bookshop in downtown Toronto between Dundas and Shuter streets, had a breakdown. He told his lawyer to draw up a complete power of attorney for Roy. The lawyer objected that Roy was too young and that he would ruin his father, but old Mr. Britnell said that things couldn't be worse than they were, and that anyway he had no alternative.

The store occupied three successive locations in the one block on Yonge Street between Dundas and Shuter streets, two on the east side, one on the west; then it moved to the new uptown centre at Bloor and Yonge. The founder, and his son and grandson after him, have all believed that a bookseller should own his building, not rent it. The old-fashioned feeling of total commitment is part of being a good bookseller. The customer too should be encouraged to develop the habit of dropping in to see what's new, and should not be subject to the abrupt dislocations that can be caused by changes in landlords' plans.

Roy gives his father credit for introducing the concept of browsing, an old-country term for grazing, nibbling a bit of lush forage here and moving on to taste that clump of clover yonder. You have always been welcome at Britnell's to "come in and browse around." But it perhaps did not truly become a "vintage bookshop" until it moved uptown during those arid years of prohibition and occupied rented quarters in an unused beverage room while its own store was being built.

During the twenties when Britnell's was being established as a new cultural centre it was within a few steps of Lawren Harris's new

66

Studio building, and A. Y. Jackson and other artists with quarters there used to drop in often. Students used to come too, in large numbers, and if they didn't buy lavishly, except at Christmas, the foundations were being laid for life-long friendships, not only with the store and its proprietor, but with books in general. The decade between the first world war and the depression was an exciting time to be alive in Toronto, and many contemporaries of Roy Britnell have been buying books from him intermittently or regularly ever since.

The hours in a bookstore are long, and a good bookseller must also read widely and know something about all sorts of books and trends in books over and above those he can actually read himself. About twenty years ago Roy Britnell had a heart attack and was warned that he must rest more. He tried for a while but it made him bored and fretful. He soon was back to the routine of coming early and staying late. However he is a rational man, and knows that sooner or later everyone has to make room for a successor. He chose to plan a gradual takeover which would relieve him of responsibility and yet allow him to continue his own active participation, which he feels is good both for the business and for him. His elder son, David, has realized the father's frustrated dream of becoming a lawyer; the younger, Barry, has bought the shop and Roy now works for Barry. So he says at least, but actually both work for the public.

I asked Roy Britnell why he thought his store had maintained itself and grown when Tyrrell's which had seemed in some ways a bigger and more successful operation in the old days had gone to the wall. It was partly of course that there was no family tradition, but Roy blames some of Tyrrell's problems on the policy of renting premises instead of buying them, but more on the policy of diversification as opposed to specialization. William Tyrrell was an apostle of diversification; he didn't believe you could make a living by books alone. He introduced greeting cards, stationery and office supplies, and even gifts. The Britnell family felt that a bookseller must know his books and that if he did that he had no time for sidelines. The Britnells always had a big line of second-hand books out of which has developed their fine reputation for rare Canadiana, which they supply to university libraries all over the world and even to the British Museum.

During the depression years they did have a big greeting card business. They did very well with it, too, since Roy used to go to New

York after Christmas and buy up remainders which were new here and could be sold the next year at very reasonable prices. They also had a lending library for a few years, which they started to keep people coming into their store. But both of these were stop-gap measures. They wouldn't have room for such sidelines now. Their outstanding asset is their service. They will go to any lengths to get a customer a book. Even the clerks are knowledgeable and have the feeling about books that you encounter in really good librarians. You are still welcome to browse and there is no high-pressure selling; in fact there is no sales pressure at all, but a bibliomaniac is no safer in Britnell's than an alcoholic is at a political cocktail party. Books are habit-forming too, and they cost money, but the difference to your physical and mental health is immeasurable.

Our present economic system, and thus to a very large extent our social system as well, are based on private business. There are many businesses larger than the Consumers' Gas Company, and many smaller than Britnell's Bookshop, but I happen to know these two men and like them. They work hard, but I think on the whole they like what they are doing. What's more, I think they believe it to be a public service, to fill a community need. They feel they must hand it on better than it was originally. I think many of the people who work for or with them share this conviction. When you feel this way, when you feel that something important depends on you, on your contribution, large or small, you can often work well and usefully long beyond the normal retirement age. And be happy doing so.

Leisure

I am not going to work today;
I shall sit on the front steps and drink beer;
The work ethic is outmoded anyway, those night school chaps say.
This is a heavenly June, the sun is warm, and the sky is blue and clear.

We are on strike. We have disrupted the entire economy of the
        country, but we have no reason to be troubled.
They know that if they try to bring in strike breakers we will riot,
Burn down the factory, perhaps, or knock the boss about and scare
        his wife and children. Otherwise things will be quiet,
We will go back to work next week or next month or sometime and
        our wages will be doubled.

If the plant has to close, there's still unemployment insurance or
        welfare to look after our pay.
We will always be supported;
In fact we will be courted
Whenever a municipal or provincial or federal election is near.

Inside, I hate myself.

Prince of
the Church

8

Destiny

Man cannot hide what he was meant to be,
Whether you call it destiny or providence or the will of God,
Or, like the behaviourists, attribute all to the blind workings of cause
        and effect, stimulus and response.

I have seen kingly backwoodsmen, and tyrants
In little factories and shops, and revolutionists
In country schools and "inner city" tenements;
And there are saints and villains everywhere.

If you are meant to take control,
In any circle of life in which you find yourself
It will be forced upon you.

If you were meant to follow,
And through ambition, chance, connections, charm,
Unwisely or unhappily reach a greatness which you were not meant
        to bear,
You can collapse and bring down others with you,
Injuring people and causes you most loved.

If we would do the will
Of God, and so fulfil
Our perfect destiny,
Habits we must unbind
And open heart and mind
Till, seeing clear and whole, we see
What we were truly meant to be.

Paul-Emile Cardinal Léger

So far, I have been thinking about people who felt the call to power or leadership. They took up the burden assigned to them and found satisfaction, health and long life in doing so. The reeve of a small village, the minister of a small church, the boss of a lumber-camp, can do the same. And in every case they put it down only reluctantly and preferably only partially. There are others who seek to change it completely. Such a one is Cardinal Léger.

When I first heard that Cardinal Léger had resigned the arch-bishopric of Montréal and gone to Africa to found and minister to a leper colony, I thought of one of my favourite Kipling stories: "The Miracle Of Purun Bhagat." It tells of a Brahmin "so high-caste that caste ceased to have any particular meaning for him," who, as Prime Minister to a Maharajah, established schools, built roads, started State dispensaries and shows of agricultural implements, and published a yearly blue-book on the "Moral and Material Progress of the State." He even visited England, with great loss of caste. When he returned, with all sorts of honorary degrees, there was a big state dinner at which his master, the Maharajah, received the Grand Cross of the Star of India, and he himself became a Knight Commander of the Order of the Indian Empire.

Next month he disappeared. He had quietly resigned wealth and status, and taken up the begging-bowl and ochre-coloured dress of a Sunnyasi, or holy man. After all,

> "He had been, as the Old Law recommends, twenty years a youth, twenty years a fighter,—though he had never carried a weapon in his life,—and twenty years head of a household. He had used his wealth and power for what he knew both to be worth; he had taken honour when it came his way; he had seen men and cities far and near, and men and cities had stood up and honoured him. Now he would let these things go, as a man drops the cloak that he no longer needs."[50]

That is just the beginning of the story, of course. I commend it to all my readers for its study of the contemplative life of those who seek God by a path that differs from ours. It has always seemed to me that when we grow feeble or blind or otherwise helpless, we could do worse than seek a quiet hermitage where we could make our peace with the Infinite.

In one of the articles I have read since commencing this study, it was suggested that many thought Cardinal Léger, weary of the conflict and heavy demands of a large archbishopric, was merely seeking seclusion and "some minor good works" in Cameroon. I have to say that when I was reminded of the story by Kipling it was not because I believed Cardinal Léger to be exhausted in mind or body, but I did think he was sick of the materialism and pretence with which he was surrounded, and wanted to get back to the first principles of his religion. I still think that this was what he wanted to do, but I also think that he found it much more difficult than he had expected.

Born in 25th April, 1904, in Valleyfield, P.Q., thirty-three miles up the St. Lawrence from Montréal, he spent his childhood in St. Anicet, where his father ran a general store. He was a precocious lad and interested in more knowledge than he could get at the local school; his mother discovered him at the age of eight, "debating burning political issues before a mirror."[51] Although his health was frail, he decided early in life that his vocation was the arduous work of the mission field; perhaps "the ruling passion conquers reason still,"[52] and he has always secretly cherished this first dedication. When he was twelve he enrolled in the minor seminary at Ste. Thérèse, some forty miles northwest of Montréal, and at twenty-one entered that city's major seminary. Ordained at twenty-five, he joined the Sulpician order which had done so much for Canada in the early years of our history. He became professor of philosophy at the seminary in Issy, France, and studied canon law in Paris, travelling during his vacations and coming in contact with the social problems which were beginning to exercise the minds of all thoughtful people, particularly young people.

When he came back to Canada in 1933, he believed it was but for a brief visit. He had promised Cardinal Verdier, then Archbishop of Paris and Superior General of his order that he would return to France. He was wrong. "I will release you from your promise to Cardinal Verdier," said his provincial superior in Montréal. "You are going to establish a seminary in Japan. The Bishop of Fukuoka expects you in the fall."[53]

It must have been a terrible undertaking, but I find few references to it in popular stories of the Cardinal's life. It might have been the fulfilment of a childhood dream; it might have been a shock from which he would not soon recover. It was like the tempering of a sword.

The only real account I have found is in the little pamphlet by Bernard Murchland, published in 1964 in a series: The Men who Make the (Second Vatican) Council, the whole of which is well worth reading. It involved five years of parish work, principally in Fukuoka, and then classes "in a small attic at the end of a long muddy road", the hygienic conditions of which, Father Léger wrote home, would "sooner or later affect the health of all of us." Yet a year later, when the seminary moved into an adequate building, and the young Sulpician director was ordered home, he could say: "I have spent six years in Japan and I leave part of my heart here."[54]

After eight years in academic and administrative work, the future cardinal became rector of the Canadian College at Rome. He had thought conditions bad for the poor in Canada, but he was appalled by what he found in Rome. A year after his appointment, now Monsignor Léger, he returned to Canada to organize the Gold Cross movement, a charitable fund which continues to this day. It has supplemented the charitable funds of the Vatican with "magnificent gifts" of "clothing, medicine, food, and other forms of aid" which might help stave off Communism, to which the poor were turning in despair. The solid base which he established in Rome made him the natural successor to the Archbishopric of Montréal when political pressures forced the resignation of Archbishop Charbonneau in 1950.

I wonder if "Le Chef", as they used to call Premier Duplessis, really felt he had profited by the change. This was no saintly martyr, no unworldly mystic. This was a man as practical and in his own way as ruthlessly determined as the great politician himself. Duplessis is said to have ruled by patronage. Léger certainly ruled by charity and Christian concern. He immediately organized the City of Charity, a refuge for the homeless and helpless. This was followed by a Home for Incurables. On January 12, 1953 he became the first Cardinal of Montréal.

It would be impossible in a sketch like this to give any comprehensive picture of Cardinal Léger's concerns for his own archdiocese and province. They are as extensive as those of a political party, but naturally very differently motivated, and he sees gradual socialization as the inevitable result of men's demands for increasing services while the increasing complexity and interdependence of life demand ever larger and more complex units for their provision and administration. His attitude towards the underdeveloped countries, as outlined by Murchland, is, however, worth quoting:

> "It is tragic that Canadians can live in peace in their abundance, that we can eat three meals a day and sleep with a clear conscience as though we were the only people in the world. We have raised a wall of egoism and indifference between ourselves and the underprivileged peoples. We no longer see what is taking place beyond the wheat curtain; we believe that everyone eats as well as we do and that famine in the world pertains to the domain of fanciful stories recounted by missionaries and explorers. We have become accustomed to considering as normal a scandalous situation. But the facts are there; we have only to open our eyes."[55]

He also says: "To contribute wheat (and Canada has lots of that) is a good thing, but to teach others how to sow their own wheat is even better."[56]

Murchland says that the focus of Cardinal Léger's thought and action is the necessity of the interior life; this is the "ultimate test of the full development of the person."[57] Only when the transcendent ideal of love illuminates his inward life can man realize his true dignity and happiness. He must have no false idols of power, prestige or wealth, no cheap happiness, easy pleasures or expedient choices. He sees Léger as a modern prophet:

> "in Joshua Heschel's words, a man who feels fiercely. God has thrust a burden upon his soul, and he is bowed and stunned at man's fierce greed. Frightful is the agony of man; no human-voice can convey its full terror. Prophecy is the voice that God has lent to the silent agony, a voice to the plundered poor, to the profaned riches of the world. . . . Prophecy protests the degradation of man, the anonymous leveling out of human existence. The prophetic voice resurrects in a relevant manner the ancient and fulfilling ideals of sacrifice, discipline, moral and spiritual achievement and the power of love and commitment."[58]

At the Second Vatican Council, which lasted from 1959 to 1965, this prophetic voice was heard again and again in support of the movements for reform and renewal. Léger would extend holiness to all the activities of daily life. To the evangelical counsels of poverty, chastity and obedience, he would add justice, humility, gentleness and mercy—"virtues of Christian life that are required of men of our time if spiritual renewal is to be effected." In my opinion these virtues are required of men of all faiths or of no faith if our world is to survive.

On his way home to Canada from one of the sessions, Léger visited tropical Africa and in particular the leper missions. After the wrangling which must have taken place, as it always does when men are discussing religion or politics (especially with no women to act as mediators and peacemakers), he was deeply impressed by the simple trust of these deformed, poverty-stricken and often hungry people. He must have felt stirrings of the old longing for the direct contact of the mission field, where, as in "The Vision of Sir Launfal" Christ tells the old knight sharing his "crust of mouldy bread" with the leper, it's

> "Not what we give but what we share,
> For the gift without the giver is bare;
> Who gives himself with his alms feeds three, —
> Himself, his hungering neighbour, and Me."[59]

But he was not free to follow this vision. The responsibilities of princely command tied him down. Instead, he established *Fame Pereo*, an organization whose Latin name, signifying "I perish by famine", shows its intent to fight world hunger. In 1968 this organization "distributed charities valued at $220,000 to 35 centres in 18 African countries" and 18 tons of medical supplies and clothing. The organization has "supplied subsidies to hospitals and dispensaries, distributed milk to undernourished children and even given help in digging wells."[60]

But while the projects and institutions he had founded prospered, the Cardinal himself was ill at ease. Some say he had a "crisis of conscience." The autumn of life, like its spring, is a time of inner turmoil. Six years of discussion in the four sessions of the Vatican Council over what seemed so plain. Separatism causing hate and violence at home in a society still dominated by greed and selfish materialism. How had he failed? What witness could he bear? People would listen to him, agree with him, praise him, and even give money to his charities, but they would not change. They would not give themselves. People kept the windows of their souls closed, as Dr. Wilder Penfield might say, for fear there would be a draft which would make them uncomfortable. If the Synod of Bishops in 1967 made little progress in the directions he thought essential, that would intensify his dissatisfaction. It might even be a dissatisfaction with himself and with his work. Was it too materialistic, too controversial? Was it destroying his own inner life?

He had discussions with the Pope, of course, and I suppose only the two of them know all that was said there. But I like to feel that God made a direct revelation to this modern prophet of the witness he was to bear as He did to Moses in the burning bush and to Paul in the blinding light on the way to Damascus. For I believe that if the heart is open, the way will always open too.

At any rate, by December of Centennial year, Paul-Emile Cardinal Léger had resigned the archbishopric of Montréal, and gone to Africa as a "simple missionary" to the lepers.

It didn't turn out to be as simple as it sounded. When anyone moves to a new community in a new environment there are going to be problems of food, water, climate. In missionary work there are also likely to be inadequacies in accommodation. In this case there was a further difficulty, in that the new missionary was a prince of the church. As Weekend Magazine put it,[61] "It is not enough to simply hang your red robe behind a curtain in your room and don a plain white cassock. To obey, after you have commanded, is not an easy thing." It is not an easy thing at all for those who must give the commands.

Léger himself has never confirmed the news stories which said that at first he encountered some jealousy and suspicion. Local officials said the government's own facilities were adequate and it didn't need anyone "coming here to tell us what to do." It would be expecting superhuman selflessness to think such problems would not be encountered, and that certain "artificial delays" and "administrative tangles" would not result.

But the new missionary persisted, patiently, humbly, but determinedly. He lived among the lepers of two colonies. He travelled some 1,300 miles confirming 4,000 children and adults. The tour lasted for "eight weeks of bitterly exhausting travel, getting up at five each morning, slogging along perilous jungle roads in the midst of the oppressive heat and humidity of the rainy season."[62] There was a special trip to Sangmélima, a leper village a hundred miles from his headquarters, about which Monsignor Nkou, bishop of that area, had told Léger. Before he could do what he really wanted to do he had by such means to discover the "African reality" and learn his "African lesson."

He came back in October, 1969, to receive the Order of Canada, an honorary degree from Waterloo Lutheran University, and a $50,000 Centennial award from the Royal Bank of Canada for his "life of devotion to the common man." A number of dignitaries met him at the airport, and afterwards, before the TV cameras in the V.I.P. Lounge, as was noted in the press, J. H. Coleman of the Royal Bank made a long speech, mostly about the Bank and its award, and little if anything about Léger and his work. Furthermore he made it entirely in English, without apologies, to a French-speaking ecclesiastic, returning to a French-speaking city from mission work in a part of Africa where French is commonly spoken by educated people. Sometimes I think we ought to send missionaries to each other before it is too late. Perhaps it is something Cardinal Léger might undertake when he retires.

When he really retires, I mean. For he is still a prince of the church and a master of men. He speaks of the "obstacles to effective action" which "have been erected by the white man's greed":

> "Slavery, colonialism, apartheid, the desire for profit and overweening conceit in the colour of our skin. We must therefore go out to them in great humility."[63]

He is as undeterred by the hideous aftermath of greed, by the poverty, hunger, sickness, over-population and general lack of resources, as he was by the apathy, disillusionment, prejudice, anticlericalism and alienation of youth which he discovered in his archdiocese.

He has not, however, become the simple missionary of his dreams. One of his first undertakings was the care, shelter and nourishment of the leper village of Sangmélima, recommended to him by Monsignor Nkou. By April, 1972, a non-denominational organization he set up in Montréal a couple of years earlier had completed 193 projects, valued at over six and a quarter million dollars, and had 9 large-scale projects and 89 smaller ones under way at an estimated value of $7,800,000. In less than ten months they had shipped 170 tons of material, and had a staff of 163 persons working full time in Montréal and Africa. Their small projects were exceptionally varied, including three medical scholarships to Ghanaian students, an elementary school for 1,500 children in Cameroon and a 70-bed bush clinic in Gabon.[64]

In April, 1972, he was seeking funds to complete a school for handicapped children, including polio victims, in Yaoundé, which Cardinal Léger and his Endeavours, his latest charitable fund, were building in partnership with the Canadian International Development Agency. It was to have a dispensary, classrooms, dormitories, workshops, and physiotherapy clinics, modern equipment and specialized staff.

Amid all these massive undertakings he still has time, however, to move about among the leper colonies, to watch the children at their play, to warm the poor forgotten ones with a sunny smile, and give courage to the frightened by the touch of a friendly hand.

As one young African nun put it:

"The Christians here had heard of a cardinal without ever dreaming they could see one. A cardinal is too near the Pope to bother with individuals. And yet . . . now, thanks to Cardinal Léger who offers himself to the humblest among us, they feel they actually know the Pope."[65]

You don't have to see the Queen every day, and all of you can't touch her hand or even catch her eye, but you know she's yours when she passes among you.

No! Cardinal Léger is not just a simple missionary. Cardinal Léger is doing in Africa what he is uniquely fitted to do, and hardly anyone else is fitted to do at all.

I am reminded of John Buchan's magnificent "The Path of the King".[66] Aristocrats, he says, are more apt to pass on the fire in their blood, that originally made them great, through the younger son with his way still to make; "the dago who blacked my boots at Vancouver may be descended by curious byways from Julius Caesar. . . . The spark . . . may smoulder for generations under ashes, but the appointed time will come, and it will flare up to warm the world."

His book tells the story of a torque worn by a young Viking prince, sole survivor of a battle in enemy territory. It was cut down to a ring by one of his descendants in a famine year, but was always worn and passed on because it carried with it a legend of royal birth. It was preserved strangely, moved from France to England and thence to America, and was lost in a western creek where little Abe Lincoln was trying to catch a fish to tempt his dying mother's appetite. He went to her in tears, but she told him it wasn't needed any longer.

The day of the seekers had past. The finder had come. It was the
Appointed Time.

In this time of racial friction and international disequilibrium
Cardinal Léger may have found his Appointed Time in Africa. And
in that case, whether or not it's what he thought he wanted or what
he thought he ought to do, doesn't really matter to us or to him. It is
his fulfillment.

Seeds of Eden

Where men have sown the seeds of fear and hate
And justified suspicion, these will grow
Quickly, deep-rooted, tough; and we, too late,
Will pluck the poison that we did not sow.

But when we see and try to substitute
An understanding love for every man,
Slow-growing, needing care, the flower and fruit
Of life, the weeds will choke it if they can.

By love and understanding, trust is fed,
By sharing rest and labour, tears and mirth,
Until the weeds of hate and fear are dead
And Eden's garden blooms again on earth.

The
Woodsman

9

Back to Earth

The clutching hands of the wind on my shoulders thrill as never the
    touch of lover;
No man has a breast as brown and tender to rest upon
As the earth lays bare to all, to uphold and succor and cover
After the racing with sun and air and water is done.

Perhaps, after resting there, we arise Antaeus-like to a new endeavour;
But there is a primitive urge that somehow it satisfies
To be one again with nature around us, for if we sever
Our ties with earth, our source of life, the spirit dies.

Who wants to live in apartments where grass is only a blur of distant
    greenery?
Who wants to breathe gasoline and hear only muffler and horn?
I want to walk under trees, not just to enjoy the scenery;
I want to hear the uncaged birds pipe up the morn.

Oh, I love the city and find it sometimes very rich and exciting,
But the hurry and pressure and competition never cease;
Often I long for natural instead of neon lighting,
And natural dark for natural rest, and work, and peace.

Roy Ivor

When I had finished thinking about Cardinal Léger, I stopped to review the ground I had covered. It seemed to me that, after my first attempt to analyze the durable qualities of Dr. Penfield, I had devoted all my attention to those whose strength showed in their dealings with masses of people.

There is another kind of strength which is equally important. It works with individuals, and sometimes it works in solitude. It is less spectacular than political or administrative leadership, and therefore it is more difficult to get information about the people who wield it. It is easier to get information about the causes for which they work or their creative achievements than it is about the men or women themselves.

One knows well enough that such people are still busy and happy, on farms, in small towns, in arduous but unnoticed service, in creative achievement. They show a different kind of courage, a different kind of determination. Some of them are not even motivated by a love for people, as are most of the busy, happy people we know.

One of the secrets of a good life certainly seems to be to keep some sort of contact with the soil—preferably your native soil. Or with the water, for I have seen fishermen with the same air of weary contentment that develops around farmers or foresters or gardeners who take their work for granted and to whom it is a way of life, not merely a way of making a living. Roy Ivor of Erindale is one of the most interesting of these.

Mr. Ivor has lived so long with birds that sometimes he seems almost like a bird himself—a heron perhaps, the "wildwood nobility" of which has always impressed observers. As the late Wm. Perkins Bull remarks in "From Hummingbird to Eagle", "It stalks with silent dignity across mud-flats or stands motionless" and, if disturbed, rises slowly and gracefully in a rush of great wings.[67]

Born on a farm in Strathroy, Ontario, in 1880, Roy Ivor was taken by his parents, when he was two years old, to a prairie farm near Moose Jaw, Saskatchewan, which was then teeming with wild life. Here, at the age of ten, he was the first to discover the nest and eggs of Richardson's merlin or the western sparrow-hawk. In 1897 the family moved back to Toronto where Ivor developed a stone and marble business. When his banker-father died in 1928 he sold the property and the business and built a cottage on a small farm on the Credit, where he cared for his mother until she died at the age of 105.

On this forty-acre property, which was eaten into by rising living costs until it was reduced to the three acres immediately surrounding the cottage, Roy Ivor came to know birds as well as most of us know people. It was a delightful spot for a sanctuary, with open woods, meadows and the lovely Credit River flowing by.

In the early 1930s, when Dr. Bull was gathering material for his book on birds, a news story told of an albino robin being cared for in the Ivor sanctuary. The two men got acquainted and Mr. Ivor furnished several stories of his birds. He was not an academically trained naturalist, but Dr. Bull was not an academically trained historian. Although material was supplied to the author and advice offered by many well known scientists, he felt that "a rigid scientific treatment would not afford a really rounded and living picture of the birds,"[68] and Mr. Ivor warmly agreed.

Thus it was in "From Hummingbird to Eagle" that there first appeared the sad love story of the blue jays, Lady and Uno, told subsequently many times by journalists but never as well until Mr. Ivor himself told it in his delightful book "I Live with Birds."[69] Dr. Bull's book also contains the first printed account I have been able to find of the chickadee that hid its sunflower seed in the buttonhole of the naturalist's coat, told again, more fully of course, in his own book. "I Live with Birds" repeats the story of the albino robin's willingness to mate with brown and red birds, but does not repeat the description that Mr. Ivor gave Dr. Bull: "more delicate than the normal robin" with "weaker, more brittle wing and tail feathers."[70]

For years scholars regarded Roy Ivor's work with half-kindly, half-amused tolerance. He was not dismayed. He really loved birds and wanted to understand them. They had to be fed first, and though he now has regular contributions of food from four large firms, there was a time when he sometimes went hungry himself to feed them. He has always regarded with some cynicism the dicta of "Authority," as he calls it, since he believes you see only fright behaviour until birds become so accustomed to you that they think of you as one of themselves and behave naturally.

An often quoted incident is his disproof, by field demonstrations, of the conclusions of certain Cornell experiments in their laboratory of ornithology. The Cornell people thought they had proved that "a songbird could not hear the human voice because it was pitched in too low a key."[71] He took the visitor who was questioning him on the subject out of his cottage. There he "took a mealworm from one of his cultures and said 'Joey, come and see what I have for you.' Like a flash (from a hundred feet away) Joey (a bluebird) came streaking to him. Mr. Ivor kept his hand closed around the worm, and when Joey could not find it, he flew to one of the cultures, looked down at the burlap covering and then at Mr. Ivor. Of course Joey got his worm and away he went. Then Mr. Ivor in his usual normal voice called various other birds by name and they all responded individually. It seemed to me to be a practical demonstration of how inconclusive scientific findings can be."[72] A similar anecdote in Mr. Ivor's own reminiscences has to do with his identification of a pair of magpies which had been frightened from their nest. When someone called to ask if a pair nesting twenty-five miles away were his, he identified them by calling the name of the female, who immediately flew down and greeted him.

When a Harvard professor declared publicly that "there is no experimental evidence whatsoever of anything remotely resembling reasoning power in birds" Mr. Ivor indignantly denied the statement and challenged the expert to visit the Windinglane Sanctuary and see for himself. He similarly denied the statement of "Authority" that "There is remarkably little outside the standard pattern of behaviour for any given species. There would appear to be little free will or choice of conduct." According to Ivor, there are differences in fear and trust, fidelity, responsibility, pugnacity, compassion, and even reasoning of a simple sort, as well as fancies regarding food, bathing-dishes, nesting-sites, etc. Some birds have a sense of humour, and many have a capacity to give and receive affection among themselves or with men and women.

As the years passed appreciation of Roy Ivor's work grew and spread. People came from hundreds of miles away to bring injured birds for his healing care or sent them by all sorts of conveyances. If he could cure them and send them out to live a natural life he did so; otherwise they remained as members of the Windinglane family. Volunteers joined him, including several graduate veterinarians, who contributed their services free in time of need. In 1948 he warned against DDT, fourteen years before Rachel Carson wrote "Silent Spring." He was honoured by the Upper Canada Zoological Society "for outstanding and meritorious service in the field of wild life and conservation" and by the Ontario Society for Prevention of Cruelty to Animals. As a result of numerous articles written by and about him, including several in the National Geographic Magazine, his name is known throughout North America and Britain, and recently he was recognized in Russia for his studies on "anting" a peculiar bird habit that he describes fully in his book along with the equally curious habit of sun-bathing.

Roy Ivor never taught his birds tricks, as a very perceptive journalist, Robert Collins pointed out a few months ago in *Weekend Magazine*; "he simply let their lives mingle with his. Sometimes they picked up human tastes; a vireo, for instance, learned to love radio music and developed a unique mixture of vireo song combined with the classics."[74] Rajah, his golden eagle, used to go for walks with him. Occasionally some of the songbirds helped him to feed the orphan nestlings of whom there were always too many in the breeding season. They were all different. He didn't blame the predators; they were following the laws of their nature. He didn't blame parents for refusing to feed a paralyzed or blind youngster; they knew it was defective and couldn't survive. He was a very permissive guardian. All he wanted was to minister to them and understand them.

Then in 1970 tragedy struck. In Christmas week Roy Ivor's bird sanctuary and home were destroyed by fire. Firemen, called by someone who saw the blaze in the middle of the night, arrived to find the ninety-one-year-old naturalist in his bare feet in the snow with a blanket over his shoulders. His first thought had been to let out all the birds he could but a hundred or more perished, including Morley the bald eagle and Casey the talking crow. He also lost his entire library, and many of his notes.

If Ivor had been an ordinary man that would have been the end of everything. When people have something to do that is worth doing and have faith in it and in their own power to accomplish it, the way opens amazingly. Already fate had been kind to Roy Ivor in bringing him an assistant who shares his empathy for wild things. She had brought a dying crow to Erindale which Ivor had brought back with his own mixture of special food and "tender loving care," and then later another, discovered and brought to her attention by the first. Then she had begun helping part time, then full time. There was some one to carry on his work. And his neighbours rallied round. Funds began to come in. The news spread, and total strangers began to contribute. By April of 1971 Mr. Ivor was back in a trailer, setting up feeding stations, since it was almost time for the spring migrations.

But there are plans for a permanent structure and, what both Mr. Ivor and Mrs. Inman would like, a combined bird observatory and hospital school.

This spring two friends of mine were driving out to the Ivor sanctuary, and invited me to go along with them. It had been raining, and the ground was wet, but Mrs. Nunes-Vaz had telephoned to say we were coming, so we thought it best to go. It was beautiful but soppily, squashily wet underfoot. We were fortunate to meet Mrs. Inman at the entrance to what is truly a winding lane, up hill and down, rough under foot (it would obviously have been impassible for a car) and no shorter for the number of turnings. About half way along it we met Mr. Ivor himself. He had come down to meet Mrs. Inman who had brought a bag of groceries that he thought he should help her to carry. As soon as we reached our destination and had set the groceries inside, he began to introduce us to his bird family with all the enthusiasm of a boy.

With old age creeping up on him, as surely it must be at ninety-three, even on him, and with what must be limited resources, his only worry is about his birds. I'd certainly like to see him get the kind of bird hospital he wants and needs. It would crown his life. But perhaps the love and trust of his birds have already done that.

If this never comes, or if it comes too late for Mr. Ivor, as such consummations, ironically, so often do, I don't think he'll be unhappy. Living with the birds as he has, he has come to accept the inscrutabilities of life as they do, Death from the pounce of a predator. Death from cold because a bluebird father who has worked all day feeding an orphaned brood doesn't know enough to cover unfeathered nestlings with his wings by night. Death at the beak of the mother albino robin as the nestlings emerge. There are so many tragedies that we achingly feel that we might have prevented. But we cannot sit and grieve. There are so many other empty mouths to fill, so many other broken bodies to heal. We don't hate birds because some are careless or greedy or jealous or pugnacious. We think only how many are beautiful and how they soar and sing and play and work and love. And we know that we must feel about people the same way. Perhaps the makeshift quarters Mr. Ivor can give his birds and the hand-to-mouth way they live are closer to what was intended than the spit-and-polish military atmosphere of many hospitals and the plush, cushiony atmosphere, both physical and mental, of an increasing number of schools. At any rate this gentle, quiet, easy-moving woodsman will make the best of them. Living with nature has taught him to live easily with both life and death.

Except as Little Children

We speak of the forest in terms of worth,
    Area, ownership, care and waste,
While the great trees stand with their roots in earth
    And offer us joys we do not taste.

We speak of the summer in terms of heat,
    Moisture and promise for crop and herd,
Nor feel the grass astir at our feet,
    Nor share the glee of the singing bird.

God, Whose kingdom only a child
    May enter, we come back to Thee;
Make us wild as the flowers are wild,
    Make us free as the waves are free.

Let us reach for the gilded moon
    Hanging low in the sweet spring sky;
Let us sleep in the sun at noon
    Or watch the miraculous ants go by.

Let us sing with our brother trees
    Of a magic older than walking men;
Let us dance with our sister breeze,
    And let wonder come into our hearts again.

The Recreationists 10

Back to Work

> My muscle's hard, my back is still unbent,
> My cheeks are ruddy from the wind and sun,
> And when I furl my sails after a run
> Across the bay, I wonder where time went.
> Always the slopes of snow to me present
> A challenge; soon my skis and I are one
> In leaping flight, and when the day is done
> I come home filled with a supreme content.
>
> How excellent would be this life of mine
> If I could spend it all so joyously,
> But I have work that I am bound to do
> To live, am tied to this production line,
> That stuffy desk. Thank God, when work is through
> Evenings and weekends all belong to me!

Harry & Helen Mole

There are many couples I know or know of, from His Excellency our Governor-General and Mrs. Michener down, whose approach to old age might well be studied together but none as interesting to me as Harry and Helen Mole. And certainly few of whom I am fonder.

They have never seemed to me competitive, never ambitious in a worldly way. They have lived comfortably, but not ostentatiously. When Harry retired from his job with the Canada Life Assurance Company at the accepted time, everyone was amazed thinking him about ten or fifteen years too young. When they rented their charming little home between Bayview Avenue and Rosedale in Toronto and moved to the country, a good many were still more amazed for both of them were deeply involved in many activities. Yet it was really not surprising if their friends had stopped to think about their way of life.

It always seemed to me that Harry Mole was one of the hundreds of thousands of people who had settled into a job and done well at it without any particular commitment. This is not undesirable in a large company. A small retailer will not accomplish much if he is not fully committed to his work, but if everyone who worked for Canada Life tried to assume extra responsibilities the resulting confusion can be imagined.

Furthermore Mr. Mole was an outdoors man. He told me once that as a high school boy during the first world war he had spent a couple of summers working on a farm, making fifty dollars the first year and seventy-five the second. Then he got a "real job" in the city, but he always remembered those two summers, and always longed for a country home. But he had been born in Toronto and this seemed to be the place where job opportunities offered themselves. He didn't marry but spent most of his spare time in sports. Then the second world war broke out, and he was wild to get into the Air Force. Somehow he managed it, but for administration not for air crew. He was in Ottawa, living out of barracks at Britannia Beach, when he met Helen Humphries.

Helen's father was in the civil service, and she herself was patriotically employed in the offices of the British Inspection Board which was checking munitions and supplies. She was also living at Britannia Beach and she was as keen on outdoor life as the young flying officer.

They knew each other only for a couple of months before his commanding officer cabled from London, England, for him to come over immediately, but things move quickly in time of war, and when he left she had promised to wait for him. Arrived in London, he was seconded to Air Ministry Intelligence in Whitehall and remained for four and a half years. He became successively Flight Lieutenant and Squadron Leader, but according to him the only significant change was that he could get pineapple juice in the mess and had a driver who always happened to be near a NAAFI place at tea-time. Harry Mole was never one to take himself too seriously.

Eventually the war ended and they were married and settled down in Toronto. Back to Canada Life where work as claims adjuster was interesting but must have seemed somewhat pedestrian after war service. Still there was always the Royal Canadian Yacht Club. Harry was an ardent sailor, and Helen was active in ladies' Lawn Bowling at the club during the summer, serving as president for a time, and in Ladies' Five-Pin Bowling during the season. For many years she was chairman of the Ladies' Committee and spent endless hours preparing for the annual garden party, bridges, fashion shows, etc. She also took up curling and square dancing.

As they became more deeply involved in community affairs, their love of the outdoors determined many of their interests. One of the first rate-payer organizations in their municipality sprang up in their community in opposition to a huge apartment development planned for a site on Bayview which had been intended for green belt land. With her business experience and orderly mind, Helen became practically permanent secretary, while Harry was president for some years and always a leader.

Harry became a member of the East York Recreation Advisory Board, was chairman for several years, and worked on an extensive survey of park needs. He also served on the Metropolitan Toronto Planning Board, the Waterfront Advisory Board, the Metropolitan Toronto and Region Conservation Authority, the Community Planning Association of Canada (Ontario Division) and the Stratford Seminar on Civic Design. There were many meetings and a great deal of paper work, but Harry and Helen moved about among the projects being sponsored by these various bodies and were at home in them all. Helen convened the Borough Centennial Ball and has continued to work with the Anniversary Balls which have succeded it.

Other responsibilities came their way, of course. It would be useless to try to list all their activities in St. Paul's Anglican Church, and Harry was also involved in Free Masonry and Conservative party associations. They were badly missed when they left Metropolitan Toronto, but because they liked people and people liked them they have kept more closely in touch than some who have moved out to the country at considerably less distance.

To be near friends who had already bought a farm near Priceville, they moved into Farquhar Oliver's old home. They are near enough to Beaver Valley and the Blue Mountain ski hills for Harry to get the exercise he loves, and Helen has taken up snowshoeing, "from necessity" she says, "since we often have to leave our car at the road and fight our way through snowdrifts up the half-mile drive to the house."

Although the house was not neglected when they moved in, every resident has his own ideas about things. Harry has kept busy, mostly outdoors, with building repairs, painting, roofing, etc. Helen has her flowers and her vegetable garden in the summer, and interior decorating in the winter. She has always sewed exquisitely, making the most beautiful Christmas gifts for her goddaughters and others, and she has always preferred to run up something for herself if she was in a hurry for a new dress rather than to buy something she didn't really like from a shop. She enjoys having a little more time for this too.

They have retained their connection with as many as possible of the activities which they enjoyed, attending the Stratford Seminar on Civic Design shortly before Harry's seventieth birthday. Since they had not sent in their registration early enough to get a room in the motel, they came in the camper, which I think they have always preferred to any other mode of travel in any case. Starting years ago with a nine-by-nine tent, they graduated to a tent trailer, and then into a self-contained Volkswagen camper in which they have toured Canada from the Gaspé Peninsula to Vancouver Island, their longest western trip following Harry's retirement. They are currently looking for a small house trailer in which they can take even longer trips.

The greatest joy of retirement, according to Harry is "release from the compulsion of daily commuting to a fixed destination at a specific time and freedom to schedule ones own activities." At the same time, remembering the picnic suppers in their garden in Toronto, with all sorts of interesting and sometimes illustrious guests, I cannot help feeling that one of their happinesses is being more out-of-doors, and that the new house trailer will sometimes take them south away from snowshoes and snow ploughs. They are as busy as ever—they could not help being busy—and there is lots of hard physical work but never a dull moment.

If people have a consuming interest in their work, they should probably continue it as long as they can do so pleasantly to themselves and profitably to what they are doing, but I have noticed that a great many farmers like to retire in the city and vice versa. The change is good, if people can adjust to it without difficulty, but they are more likely to do so if they have a fair amount of preparatory experience. I have known farmers fretting themselves to death in town and city-dwellers working themselves into heart attacks when they undertook outdoor work and exercise for which a completely sedentary life had not prepared them. To me, Harry and Helen Mole seem an outstanding example of a couple who knew what they wanted in life and got as much of it as they could without hurting others or themselves. They are still young of course, by my standards, but they both seem as well as ever, and certainly as cheerful, active, fun-loving and thoughtful.

Off the Treadmill

I always thought that I would spend old age
    Doing the things I had not tried before,
Not having time, but now I find somehow
    I do not want to do them any more.

If I had worked somewhat less earnestly
    At making money, but had learned to play,
Time might not, so interminably long,
    Stretch out before me as it does today.

The Creative Artist 11

The Purple Moment

Of course the snow is purple —
Or blue or green —

Everything around is coloured, gay or sombre,
And the colours change constantly
As the earth moves and the winds and the shadows.

That's why a photograph is dead, even a colour photograph,
Even by the greatest photographer with the finest equipment.

The artist has to give us the feeling that this is one moment,
Vital, exquisite, terrible,
Snatched from time and yet with a permanence,
Never to be repeated.

He has to put something of his own life into it,
His passion for beauty or strength or stillness,
His love of colour and line and texture,
His love of country,
His love of God.

A. Y. Jackson

From those who find the fountain of youth out of doors, on farms, in forests or on the water, it is a natural step to those creative spirits who work in the arts. Although they are producers, they are not competitors for material profits. Many earn their livings in other fields than that which really means most to them. A. Y. Jackson says a true artist has to paint even if his works accumulate in garrets or outhouses. Writers and musicians are often the same. As for the performing arts, in spite of a few spectacular successes, life is a struggle for most, and there must be a very deep-seated love of the work for anyone to make it his or her principal interest.

There are a dozen senior people in the creative field whom I know personally as contemporaries or whom I would like to know. Dora Mavor Moore is one. Earle Birney is another. So are Gordon Sinclair and Joe Morgan—may they both forgive me for coupling their names. The great Fridolin has not yet reached the age of retirement, although he is in his sixties; in any case he will never be old. We have recently lost several distinguished musicians by death, but there are others who are still active and significant. I have, however, chosen A. Y. Jackson as my prototype. Partly because he was a member of the Group of Seven, striking innovators in their day, whose work I have been seeing since I first visited one of their earliest exhibitions as an undergraduate. Partly also because he has an association with East York, my home borough, through a friend who was active in public life here. For twenty-five years, when the late Walter Stewart occupied the house where I now live, its walls were covered with A. Y. Jackson pictures, as I shall note presently. I can still imagine them here, and, though I have only met the artist casually, I cannot help thinking of him as an old friend.

Alexander Young Jackson, to give him his full name, is perhaps the "grand old man" of the creative arts in Canada today. At the age of ninety they tell me he is still often to be found in the quarters specially prepared for him four years ago at the McMichael Galleries near Kleinburg. While I was assembling the final manuscript of this book I saw him at the opening of the most recent addition to the Galleries, sitting in a corner surrounded by admirers, celebrity hunters and autograph hounds. He spends some time in a nursing home but still gets to many functions. He looked tired but happy,

94

and so he should be. He is in safe harbour after a tempestuous life, amid many fine examples of his own work and the work of his old friends.

The boyish carefreeness and *joie de vivre* commented on at the time of his Retrospective Exhibition in Toronto[75] twenty years ago are less evident today but the friendly nonchalance and interest in people, especially the young, are still a part of him. It is through this interest in younger people that he became a familiar figure in East York. In his autobiography[76] he mentions a young man who came to him seeking an interview for *Varsity*, the student newspaper. This was Walter Stewart, back from the First World War to finish his education, who must have called on Jackson soon after the latter was released from War Records. Jackson liked Stewart's "intelligent questions" and "good article" and later met him again in Hart House where the young man was conducting an equally successful interview with the poet W. B. Yeats. The acquaintance ripened into friendship.

> "his wife, Jane, was also interested in art and literature. As the family came along I was Uncle Alex to all of them. . . . The Stewart home is a kind of private gallery, with Jackson paintings in every room."[77]

Walter Stewart was one of the founders of the East York Kiwanis Club, the first Chairman of the combined Board of Education, and the first chairman of the Library Board. Naturally A. Y. Jackson pictures went into the new High School, the Public Library, and eventually the collection of the East York Foundation. Walter and Jane are both gone now, and most of their Jackson collection is in the McMichael Galleries, but I came to know them very well during their later years, and they told me many tales of the great painter, his unassuming modesty, his self-depreciation, and yet his fighting spirit when he was talking of things he believed in. I have found all these confirmed in his autobiography.

Although both his paternal and maternal grandparents had been prosperous, Jackson's father was no business man. He failed in several ventures, and when his family would no longer back him he deserted his wife and children. Thus young Alex had to contribute to the family exchequer as soon as he finished public school. By that providence which somehow seems to shape our lives, he got a job as an office boy with a lithographing company. He was only twelve at the time, but before too long he was noticed, while waiting for errands, making drawings which seemed remarkable for one of his age. He was transferred to the art department where he became assistant to a bilingual and widely-read lithographer, "steeped in the classics, biography and history". After six years, however, young Jackson's salary was still only six dollars a week, and he moved on to a printing-house, then a photo-engraving house, and finally to another lithographer.

All this while, Jackson was helping his family, and attending night school and later William Brymner's art classes. In 1905 he and his brother worked their way to Europe on a cattle ship along with a stonemason who could "recite Shakespeare by the hour" and a big Swede with a considerable knowledge of art. It is amazing how many times Jackson finds kind things like this to say about casual acquaintances. He saw the best in almost everyone.

He did not remain in Montreal long after his return from Europe. There was a lithographers' strike, and he went to Chicago, where he renewed his acquaintance with his father, worked for a firm of designers and studied four nights a week at the Art Institute. By 1907 two more of the family at home had grown old enough to help, and he had saved enough money to study in France. The cost of living in Europe in those days was very low, and he managed to stay for two and a half years.

One of the first canvases Jackson painted in Canada after his return in 1910 was "Edge of the Maple Wood", which was to appear in the 1912 exhibit of the O.S.A., after another year of work and another year in France, and to bring him into touch with the young Toronto artists who were later to become the Group of Seven. It was bought by Lawren Harris, whose grandfather had been one of the founders of the Massey-Harris company. Harris, with his friend Dr. James MacCallum, a patron of the arts, was constructing a studio building, in Toronto. Here, after spending the summer painting from the homes of friends in the Georgian Bay area, Jackson, guaranteed by MacCallum, rented a studio and set out on a full-time winter of painting. Tom Thomson, under similar encouragement, shared a studio with him. They moved in early in January, 1914, full of enthusiasm for the north country and for putting independent life into Canadian art.

When war was declared Jackson did not enlist at once. He was not a warlike nor even a highly competitive man, but after news arrived of the Battle of St. Julien,[78] he felt the time had come to enlist.

Wounded in the shoulder, he was transferred to Canadian War Records where he remained until 1919. When he was demobilized he returned to his studio in Toronto. The next year the Group of Seven was organized "to interpret Canada and to express, in paint, the spirit of our country."

Writing of the early days of the Group, John A. B. McLeish speaks of Jackson's "forthright personality",[79] "fine depth and spirituality".[80]

> "His sojourns in Brittany and Provence, and in London and Rome, had matured and steeped his techniques without perverting his essential at-oneness with nature in Canada, a communion which he maintained with a singular purity and devotion through the course of a long, active life."[81]

Even to a painter like Jackson, most of whose work had been done in lower and more settled country, the Georgian Bay, Muskoka and northernmore parts of Ontario, were fascinating. The brilliance of the light, the boldness of the rock formations, the masses of wild flowers and foliage, and the network of little waterfalls, rivers and lakes, still largely untouched by man, seemed to demand new and freer treatments. But these did not find ready acceptance in a public just emerging from its pioneer stage. Art lovers and critics looked for the muted tones and pastoral scenes established as the norm in another climate and country. They had not yet learned to think for themselves. The Group was severely criticized.

The Group members were not inarticulate. Lawren Harris declared, in the foreword to the 1922 catalogue of their first separate exhibition, that you coudn't "depict the autumn pageantry of our northern woods with a lead pencil." Lismer in an essay "Canadian Art" pointed out:

> "Canada has not the traditional pastoral quality of the older countries. It is rugged and stern over large areas, untamed— perhaps untamable. Its seasons are not the gentle passive gliding of one into the other; they are distinctive and extreme in contrast. . . . no timid play of subtleties, but bold and massive design."[82]

Jackson spoke even more strongly. No one had worked harder than he; no one had sacrificed more for his art.

> "Some of us spent years of study in the art schools of Paris, London, or Antwerp. Some of us won medals. Some of us

exhibited in the salons and academies. . . . We have spent weeks in the bush, camping until the snow drove us out; lived in tents and shacks and trailed all over the north country to find out how to interpret our own country in terms of art, and it is somewhat discouraging to find that one who has spent all his time in Toronto, not an artist, but a newspaperman, should know so much more of the subject than any of us."[83]

The artist went on to suggest that after Mr. Hector Charlesworth, editor of Toronto's distinguished weekly "Saturday Night", and the most uncompromising critic of the Group, had finished rearranging the National Gallery in Ottawa, he might be lent to New York to "straighten out" the Metropolitan, and noted how many of the artists Mr. Charlesworth was holding up as models had, in their day, been considered dangerous innovators: Constable, Turner, Courbet, Monet, Whistler or Cézanne.

Those days of controversy had no more exciting moment than the debate at the Empire Club between Sir Wyly Grier, the well-known portrait painter and representative of the old school, and Alex Jackson representing the Group of Seven. Jackson, in his usual self-effacing way, passes it over almost in silence, using it merely as a lead-in to his Arctic Holiday with Dr. Banting.

"It was a friendly debate in the course of which Grier contended that the painters of the Group of Seven were moving away from the country that people were familiar with (it was said somewhere that they would discourage immigration), and were going farther and farther north so that he believed our final objective must be the North Pole. . . . I asked myself, 'Well, why not?' Shortly afterwards I wrote to the Minister of the Interior . . . that I should like to make a painting of the most northerly post in the world."[84]

McLeish in his book on Lismer, however, devotes six pages to the debate, quoting extensively from both speakers, Jackson being then in his young prime:

"Jackson was always a debater of great power, he always moved directly and vividly to the main points at issue; he knew how to be simple and picturesque where those qualities counted most; his sincerity was compelling; and the cumulative effect of his vivid language and reasoning was almost overwhelming."[85]

Jackson insisted that the older European artists whose works were extensively copied here could never truly express the pioneering spirit of Canadians, which was challenged by the rugged landscapes and raw colours of the Canadian wilderness. You couldn't make up a Canadian art show only, or even mainly, of "portraits of contented farmers, industrial sites, and unmortgaged farms," any more than you could "tie the poet up in the barnyard and have him write odes on pure-bred stock."

> "Art is what makes a nation articulate, not alone painting, but literature, drama, music, sculpture and architecture, and every great nation must create these things for itself. Art is the voice of a nation speaking through time. A nation does not speak through its blue-books. . . .
>
> "There is another thing to consider. We cannot go on depending more and more on the States for our literature, drama, and all kinds of art, and create nothing for ourselves without losing our identity, or—or, if it ends up as a mere economic identity, will we be distinguishable from Americans? . . .
>
> "There are lots of people who can give an impetus to creating things Canadian . . . but they say it won't pay. Well, a few artists, with no capital and few friends, started a movement which the British press says breathes the spirit of Canada and not one of them asked if it would pay."[86]

No artist has ever, probably, known Canada better or loved her more than A. Y. Jackson. He painted tirelessly, from coast to coast. The chapters in his autobiography bear such titles as: Quebec, Camping and Canoeing, Jasper and Skeena, An Arctic Holiday, Second Arctic Voyage, Painting in the West. His recollections are full of the people he met and for each he has a kind or admiring word. He notes older people's ages—this book was published in 1958 when the author was already seventy-six himself—and remarks that Emily Carr did her greatest paintings after she was 58, and that when her heart prevented her from continuing to paint she turned to writing. When he was visiting a radium mine in the Great Bear Lake area he met J. B. Tyrrell, the famous geologist, who was going on to

Coppermine to celebrate his eightieth birthday. In the end Alex Jackson may outdo them all.

He has had a great zest for life and a great love of Canada and he has gone to places because he wanted to see and understand more, but he does not say all artists should do so. What they must do is see things for themselves wherever they are. He recognizes the inadequacy of the rewards for painting, and wonders why any one should devote his life to it. But: "The answer is simple; the true artist cannot help himself."

> "Artists would continue to paint even if they had no sales at all; a creative urge impels them. Lismer used to boast that he possessed the largest collection of Lismers in the country, and Emily Carr's work piled up, with only occasional sales at ridiculously low prices. There were times when she could not afford canvas, and painted on wrapping paper. In spite of such impressive evidence of the lack of public interest in their work, both continued to paint, undaunted by it and by the knowledge that in Canada only the poets rank lower than the painters in the financial scale. Someone once remarked that wealthy Canadians would as soon keep a boa constrictor as support a poet."[87]

A. Y. Jackson will be contented wherever he is for the rest of his days. When the ownership of the Studio Building changed, he went to Manotick. He then was provided with a pied-à-terre at the Mc-Michael. He can see his paintings hung in every gallery in Canada. He is a figure of importance wherever he appears. He can sketch or write if, as and when he so desires. And with his mind's eye he can compose better pictures than he has ever painted and write better books, for he has the supreme gifts of love and imagination.

"Writing is not enough; there must be an audience"

The man who wrote that lied
Or did not know the inner needs
Any creative process feeds.
The writing *is* enough.

When I was five or so, through the snowy village street
In the early winter dusk, my mother and I to a house of sickness went.
She left me outside,
Saying, "Don't run away; be good."
As if I were a baby, I thought, feeling forsaken,
And walked up and down resenting it, pushing behind me each picket
            in the fence.
Then, by the simple grave rhythm insensibly overtaken,
And feeling the snowflakes chilly on my cheeks and sweet,
I rhymed the early moon indifferent.
Oh, it was childish stuff
And quite without direction or pretence;
I only knew it made me feel content,
Complete.
The singing was enough.

Tasted, the rhyme and rhythm grew to be
A sort of inner sustenance to me
But nothing saleable, for editors, like the moon,
Turned silent chilly cheeks against my tune.

Years passed.
I worked and played and slept and ate,
And knew frustration, love and hate,
But nothing important came, or, coming, seemed to last.
The counted grey hairs on my mirrored head
Grew countless, but in loneliness or trying to sleep at night,
Stretched on my narrow bed,
Always strange dream folk came and sang to me,
An agonized ecstatic hearer.
I shaped intently stories I had to write
And rounded songs out of the sharp distress
And the cold clouded mirror.
Sometimes I even wrote them down and sent
To editors, but they were always rejected.
(I come across some still in old pigeonholes and boxes where they are
            least expected,
But the ones I want most are always gone and I have no idea where
            they went.)
It didn't matter generally. My real life was inside my head.

One day, speaking harshly to a loved one, without thought,
I suddenly remembered a dream story I had wrought
Through the years, based on an essay written when I was ten
About the U.E. Loyalists, until it became a three-volume chronicle
        novel,
And I said to myself, "Ernest would not
Have done that. He went on patiently through the years letting Helen
        think she had made him happy by
Sacrificing her life to a meretricious ideal, and thinking she was
        sacrificing it to him. He was fine and tough
And so he was content to satisfy
His standards for himself. He stood erect without support of praise
        or blame or even knowledge."

And I quickly kissed the shocked surprise
From the dear querulous mouth and puzzled eyes,
Turned back the question with quick soft laughter
And went back to my work refreshed. We do what is given us to do
        in mansion or in hovel.
I had not thought of Ernest and Helen for a long time, but that night
They would come back to me amid the fallen rose-petals of a long-
        forgotten June.
What matter
If the whole world was careless as the moon
About my snowy picket-fence of verses?
What if I could not learn the modern patter,
The poignant staccato call,
That critics love, and great wits, and students at college?
A clarity of spirit came to me in singing
That stayed with me, somehow, through the wearisome hours after.
Shakespeare knew what he was talking about when he called us
        dream stuff.
The writing is enough.
It is all.

The Enthusiasts 12

Service

> I had a dream of a people united
> In friendship, and clean in body and soul,
> All working together to make the world better
>   With nothing of self in their goal.
>
> So I tried to break barriers and bring them together,
> Clear-visioned, with wisdom and love in control,
> Forgetting my fears and my fragmented weakness,
>   And suddenly found myself whole.

Rev. Richard D. Jones and Dr. Gordon Bates

Dick Jones, as he likes to be called, is a convert; for this reason he is doubly enthusiastic. Not a convert in the usual sense, however. He may well remain a Methodist at heart; he has all the glowing enthusiasm associated with the finest expression of that faith; but there is no Methodist Church in Canada today. And perhaps he has merged his denominationalism in the search for the Power that rules the universe and that should bring men together as brothers instead of separating them.

In the same way, although born in the United States, Dr. Jones became a Canadian citizen in 1957. Perhaps he thought it was time he gave some formal indication of his intention to make this his home, although he had already served on the Canadian delegation to the World Brotherhood Conference in Paris, France, in 1950, and again in Brussels, Belgium in 1955. In the same year[88] he received the Beth Sholem Brotherhood Award, and I am sure he felt as much at home with the members of the synagogue as if he had been an Israeli Jew. For this man considers all men his brothers.

Born in 1906 in Elizabeth, N.J., Dick Jones was the son of a Welsh coal-miner, from whom he doubtless inherited the small but burly figure and the resonant voice which have led some of his flock of Provincial Exchange students to nickname him "Papa Bear." I asked him once when he had first thought of becoming a clergyman, and he couldn't remember. He guessed that when, as a new infant he was put in his mother's arms, she had probably said to his father, "Well, John, there's our preacher."

At any rate he got his B.A. from Wesleyan University when he was twenty, taught Latin and English in Athens College, Athens, Greece, from 1928 to 1931, and took his M.A. in 1932 and his B.S.T. in 1934 from Boston University School of Theology. Nothing slow about this young man even then.

Ordained in the Newark Conference of the Methodist Church, he spent thirteen years in pastoral work there, several of them presumably on leave of absence, since he served during the Second World War with the Marine Corps in Northern Africa, Italy and Southern France. He has the gusto of a Marine, but the courage of a conscientious objector. Perhaps he was their chaplain.

On his return to his pastoral charge, he organized the New Jersey

Round Table of the National Conference of Christians and Jews, and later similar round tables elsewhere. In 1947 he left his ministerial work and entered full-time on his work for promotion of better human understanding as director of the Canadian Council of Christians and Jews. He became president in 1967 and is as active as ever today, with no thought or retirement, apparently in his own mind and certainly in the wishes of his staff.

Perhaps his boyhood in the industrial city of Elizabeth accounts in some measure for his ready acceptance of all groups in the community. Elizabeth had its black community, its Polish community, its Italian community. You could live on the right side of town or the wrong side. But there would be no right or wrong for Dick Jones as long as there were people needing friendship.

It must be admitted that his associates in the Canadian Council of Christians and Jews are mostly pretty well padded: they would have to be to help him much in his organization of local offices, interfaith conferences, student exchanges, interfaith camps, award banquets, publications, and so on and so on. However, or so he says, he's never tried to keep up with the Joneses. He hasn't had to; he was born one.

His travels also fitted him for his chosen field. While he was teaching in Athens, itself a broadening experience, he rode a motorcycle from Spain to Pakistan, travelling with Richard Haliburton through Iraq and Iran. Anyway it has always seemed to me that Methodists were the most open-minded of the evangelical churches, not having started as a church at all but as a group within a church, getting together only for spiritual exercises. My own upbringing in a Methodist parsonage, though circumstances had forced the establishment of a separate denomination a century and a half earlier, was completely free of all religious bias or prejudice, and I assume this held true of Dick Jones too.

At the same time this man is no woolly-headed idealist, but a very practical person. He has made interfaith things fun to do. He has made them fashionable. He has, in fact, made it difficult for anyone who wishes to be considered progressive to stand aside from his projects. At the same time he knows that churches have vested interests as well as corporations, which neither can wholly neglect at the present time. He doesn't make demands on people which they are not prepared, or are perhaps unable, to meet. I am sure he does not, for instance, expect doctrinal divergences to disappear, or wide differences in background and education to be set aside, but he does expect to secure amiable communication between groups who worship one common God, however different their means of approach—and in their actual approach to God perhaps they are not as different as they seem.

His big work, and the one on which he must count for longest-lasting effect, is with young people. I have never been at one of his interfaith camps, but I have met his exchange student groups on a number of occasions. There is a freedom and gaiety about them that augurs well for their future.

In addition to his proper work, although often associated with it, are his continued travel and contributions to many journals on the subject of human relations. He has visited almost all European countries, including Poland and Lithuania. He has also been in India, China, Mexico and Alaska. Always he has got along happily with people. If there were difficulties he made light of them. If there were problems he overcame them and afterwards they made good stories.

Naturally he has received many honours, which he bears very lightly. Besides the Beth Sholem Brotherhood Award he received the Centennial Medal for his work in Inter-group relations, and in 1967-8 was appointed Chaplain of the Metropolitan Toronto Police Department. In June, 1972, he received the City of Toronto Merit Award, and in December of the same year was appointed Officer of the Order of Canada.

We hear of organizations, similar to this one of Richard Jones', that have flourished for a while and then quietly disappeared. What makes this different? Why was this able, in 1971, to triumphantly celebrate its twenty-fifth anniversary?

Most people say Mr. Jones himself is the secret, or Dr. Jones, we should say, for he has an LL.D. in addition to all his other honours. Staff and directors agree. He is a salesman. He could sell elephants to the Eskimos or Quebec heaters in tropical Africa. He could sell high-rise development to the new men on the City of Toronto Council. He could have made money—heaps of the stuff—with that infectious enthusiasm of his. But that would have left a bad taste in his mouth, brought up as he had been and having reached the conclusions he had reached about life.

So, as he gets older, he has no regrets. He has seen the world and found it interesting. He has talked with princes without losing "the common touch". He is not one who needs a second career. He has

106

found the career which is ideally suited to his talents and tastes, and such a man can, and should, go on until he drops.

That is what Dr. Gordon Bates is doing. Like Dr. Jones, he is an enthusiast. He entered early upon a field which he made outstandingly his own in Canada, and in consequence has become internationally known as well.

In physical energy they cannot be compared, of course, for Dr. Bates was born in 1885 and so is old enough to be Dick Jones' father. He seems to have shrunk a bit since I first met him and heard him speak, but when a man is nearly ninety that is safer than being too heavy.

Dr. Bates was born in Burlington, Ontario, and educated in Hamilton, Woodstock and Toronto Medical School. Astonishingly enough, and a measure of the bounce with which he started, he took post-graduate work in political science at the University of Toronto, and in French language and literature at the Sorbonne. But his major interest always has been public health and particularly preventive work.

Although his interest has been constant, his work in the field has been varied. He has lectured in the University of Toronto Department of Medicine, directed a special treatment clinic of the Toronto General Hospital, worked as assistant pathologist at the Toronto Hospital for the Insane, as it was then called, and in the field of social disease. He has been a member and given active leadership in the Canadian Medical Association, the Canadian Public Health Association, the Ontario Medical Association, the College of Physicians and Surgeons, and the American Public Health Association. A life member of the Toronto Academy of Medicine, he is the senior holder of the Medal of Pasteur and in 1970, at the age of 85, became an Officer of the Order of Canada.

Much of Dr. Bates's work has been educational or informative. For ten years he edited the *Canadian Public Health Jouranl*, but *Health* has been one of his major interests for years. It is the voice of the Health League of Canada, of which he is vice-president and general director. I first made his acquaintance some years ago when he was seeking a subsidy for this magazine from the Metropolitan Toronto Special Grants Committee. At that time I had to oppose the grant, as health was not a responsibility of the region, and in any case I did not see how the magazine was going to be of practical use. However, I became a subscriber to it myself and even read at it, which is not true of all the magazines that come into the house. I would prefer to see Dr. Bates's still abundant energy directed into the preparation of articles for newspapers and magazines with a wider circulation among the uninformed, since *Health*, though not really a professional publication, is distributed largly to professionals. I would also like to see him associated with more educational films similar to *Damaged Lives* which was done in Hollywood and of which he was technical director.

However, *Health* goes to many doctors and dentists, and it has been a factor in reminding them and their patients of certain public health undertakings which might otherwise have been allowed to drift aimlessly. The campaign which Dr. Bates and the Health League waged for years in support of water fluoridation was a major factor in eventually bringing it to most of the major centres in Canada. The effect will be felt slowly as more and more children grow up with fluoridated drinking water. I do not suppose the dentists need fear bankruptcy, however, in view of the trash most children eat. I would like to see *Health* go into the matter of economical diets, and calorie and protein counts for food under the new metric system. Dr. Bates, however, believes that venereal disease is the major preventable health problem today, and it bothers him from a moral as well as a physical angle.

Dr. Bates is also interested in the environment and has attended a number of the meetings of the Organizing Committee for the Survival Institute of Canada. It is not precisely a health, but rather an interdisciplinary problem, in which all sorts of people are involved— naturalists, geographers, economists, planners, sociologists, educators, and ordinary people, who are after all the salt of the earth. He is a leading light of Rotary and many of his fellow members are also in this project.

He is a great asset to any organization in which he takes an interest. He has friends and acquaintances all over the world, and can command a hearing where few Canadians could.

But we can all command a hearing somewhere, and if we have ideas about a better life for everyone, whether through the removal of tensions between individuals and groups as Rev. Richard Jones hopes, or through better control of our own behaviour, as Dr. Gordon Bates believes, or through putting ourselves in harmony with our environment instead of destroying it, as I myself think is important, or whether a man or woman has an interest of his own that he would like to share with others, the years between sixty and eighty are the time to develop such interests. Even devotion to a church or a political party can keep a person younger than his or her years. Ideally this special interest should be developed before the time for retirement comes, and, since we do not all have the leadership and brains to find our own crusades, but all have a contribution to make to those in which we really believe, we should try to find a group with a leader we can trust and admire, and put our energies into it as enthusiastically as the greatest and wisest of men. We will enjoy life as much and in the same way.

Always Occupied

There are so many roads to travel,
　　So many things to see,
The world and all that's in it should
　　Enchant unceasingly.

There are so many mixed-up people,
　　I cannot see — can you? —
How anyone could sit back idle
　　With nothing left to do.

And even when barred from sight and action —
　　The realm of thought is broad —
I could spend years in contemplating
　　Eternity and God.

The Reformer

13

Free Enterprise

"My little plant," the manufacturer said
With modest pride, leading his guest by row
On row of trembling girls, who worked below
The earth-line, in his cellars. Pale as snow
The flowers in their cheeks. That was a bed
Where only livid parasites could grow.

He did not feel the cold. Rotund, well-fed,
He did not know his plant's deep roots were dead.

David Croll

It is possible to achieve the sense of fulfillment that is needed to carry us happily and efficiently into old age by becoming a productive part of society, efficiently providing useful goods and services. But society is man-made and imperfect. It needs the constant leavening influence of reformers to keep it from becoming dry or soggy. Such a one is David Croll.

Senator Croll is one of the most remarkable men I have met. He has had meteoric successes, but he has never hesitated to imperil or abandon them in support of his personal convictions. He has been too far to the left to enjoy the full confidence of his fellow Liberals at either the federal or the provincial level. On the other hand he never seems to have toyed with the idea of finding a more comfortable home with the C.C.F. or its rather different successor the N.D.P., much less with the Communists, presumably because these so-called left-wing parties approached social and economic reforms by political methods with which he was not in sympathy. Although he was a K.C. (now Q.C.) at 34, no one thinks of him as a lawyer. Although he served in the army throughout the second world war, no one thinks of him as a soldier. Although he has been in politics at one level or another almost all of his adult life, no one thinks of him as a politician. And although he was sworn in on the Talmud when he became the very young mayor of Windsor in 1930, no one thinks of him as a Jew. He is just David Croll, the champion of the oppressed.

He was himself born among the oppressed, a Jew in Moscow, in 1900, the hinge year of the century. His father, Hillel, came to Windsor, Ontario, in 1904, and two years later sent for his wife and three small sons. The father had built up a small cattle business and the mother kept a small grocery behind which the family lived. Little David, like the hero of any Alger book, laid the foundation of his fortune as a newsboy, supplementing the take by shining shoes. He was still selling papers, morning and evening, when he got into high school, but that didn't prevent him from sailing through his examinations trimuphantly with plenty of football, basketball and baseball on the side. At seventeen he made an unsuccessful attempt to join the Royal Flying Corps, then something new in the way of military effort. Failing in this, he and a friend set up a newsstand with the aid of which David put himself through law school in Toronto. By 1930 he was five years married, head of his own law firm, and mayor of Windsor.

It was a bad time for anyone to take municipal office, and nowhere worse than in Windsor. The production of motor vehicles by 1932 was just a quarter of what it had been four years earlier. What is more, the United States had forbidden workers to commute across the border, because the depression was equally bad there and they wanted to save what jobs there were for their own citizens. It sometimes seemed that everyone was "on the pogey" and taxes soared to heights which made it difficult to collect even from those who were working. Half the urban municipalities in the province came "under supervision" and Windsor was not the only formerly wealthy city to default on its bonds.

At the provincial election of 1934, Mitchell Hepburn who had spent the years since 1930 reorganizing the almost defunct and hopelessly divided Liberal party, persuaded David Croll to accept the candidacy in Windsor-Walkerville. Croll was regarded as a labour leader who, with the aid of Arthur Roebuck and Morrison McBride, would swing many labour votes across the province to the Liberals. He was elected with a smashing majority, and became Welfare Minister on the first Hepburn cabinet. He retained the mayoral chair in Windsor.

Later he also assumed the Labour Ministry, and the new portfolio of Municipal Affairs. Even a man of Croll's tireless energy must have found the combined responsibility heavy, especially in view of the economic situation, in which all three departments faced a tangled snarl of problems. And yet no one seems to have questioned Croll's administration, and indeed some needed reforms were introduced during the years between 1934 and 1937.

Early in 1937 the C.I.O. began an aggressive organizational campaign in Ontario. Their methods were unorthodox, but the times prompted them. The premier, while not unsympathetic to labour, put "economic advance and the maintenance of law and order"[89] ahead of the demands of the workers, as pointed out by his biographer, Father Neil McKenty. A sit-down strike at the Holmes Foundry near Sarnia led to violence and arrests. Hepburn warned that a sit-down strike was trespassing and would not be permitted.

On the very day the premier made this statement, Father McKenty points out, David Croll announced Ontario's first minimum wage for men.

> "Business profits were increasing, Croll explained to the House, but not wages: 'Labour feels quite rightly that it should have a stake in the returning prosperity. We fully agree.' Croll then warned: 'It takes no prophet to predict that without Government action 1937 will be a year of industrial disturbance'."[90]

It was more than an introduction to the minimum wage legislation.

C.I.O. unions were at that time regarded with grave suspicion by A.F. of L. unions as well as governments. Furthermore they were American. Hepburn made a valiant effort to keep them out of his province, but two members of his own cabinet felt that he was on dubious legal grounds. These were his attorney-general, Arthur Roebuck, and his labour minister, David Croll. The differences came to a head when the C.I.O. succeeded in striking the General Motors plant in Oshawa on a question, primarily, of union recognition. The premier demanded the resignation of Croll and Roebuck on the grounds that they were not in accord with government policy in "fighting against the inroads of the Lewis organization and Communism in general."

The resignations were handed over at once, of course, but both men continued to support the government on other matters. Croll said, if he had to choose, he would rather march with the workers than ride with the bosses; with his background he could not do otherwise. Croll also pointed out in surprisingly passionless terms:

> "the working people have a right to form their own associations for the purpose of collective bargaining . . . the privilege of joining the lawful union of their choice . . . if they, in their wisdom and in their knowledge of the conditions under which they work, consider that they should make the final resort to a strike, then that too is their right; and having struck they shall not be molested if they picket peacefully and within the law."[91]

On the surface the results of the 1937 election seemed to support Hepburn, but Croll was also re-elected, and in the end it became evident that he rather than the premier was in touch with the deeper under-currents of history. The Government had cut taxes, paid a

113

subsidy to municipalities, taken over the municipal share of old age pensions and mothers' allowances, granted the first Canadian pensions to the blind and slashed hydro rates. In all of these policies Croll had played a part. In 1935 he had launched a province-wide campaign for the adoption of children in public charge, in which the premier set a good example. In the same year his department had taken over the administration of the affairs of the Dionne quintuplets, whose interests were faithfully served in spite of many criticisms; without his intervention it is doubtful if the little girls could have survived.

After the 1937 election Croll had less interest in the legislature. War clouds were already on the horizon when he won another term as mayor of Windsor in 1938. When they broke, he enlisted promptly in the Essex Scottish as a private, and he was still His Worship Private Croll when he was entertained by the Council of the Royal Borough of Windsor in England. He was indeed marching with the workers.

His administrative ability and experience could not be wasted for long. There were training courses and promotions. When he finally came home it was as a lieutenant-colonel. Discharged in 1945, he was elected in the same year to the House of Commons for Toronto-Spadina, offering himself there at the personal request of Prime Minister King who feared that the Communist leader, Tim Buck, might carry the seat. Croll had always maintained amiable relations with King even during the years when the King-Hepburn feud was destroying the Liberal party in Ontario. He was re-elected in 1949 and 1953, and did much important work on committees and introduced much important legislation in his chosen fields, including the Fair Employment Practices Act, but in spite of his outstanding qualifications and career, he was never appointed to the cabinet.

Many people have found it hard to understand why such a man was by-passed so often in favour of lesser men. Some have suggested that it was a case of the discrimination against which Croll had always fought. I think it was rather the fact that Croll was first, last and always a reformer. The Liberal party has not really been a reform party in Canada for many years. The old British Liberalism which moved towards free action in all fields (including the removal of tariff barriers) has not been an important factor in Canadian elections, as far as I can see, since the reciprocity election of 1911. Most of the so-called reforms introduced by the Liberals have been urged on them by others whose support they needed or have been demanded by the people and the economic conditions of the country in unmistakable terms. Their major boast seems to be that they have held together the rickety structure of Confederation, and they have done this by adjusting their vessel constantly to conflicting winds and cross currents. This is no place for a serious reformer. He can rock the boat dangerously at the wrong moment, because he will not adjust himself readily to what seems expedient.

In 1955, when it looked as though Croll could no longer be ignored, he was moved to the senate. It was one of those honours which an active politician, full of fire and ideas, would happily do without. I don't know what arguments were used to induce him to accept it. Perhaps he was happy to be free from the immediate and constant party discipline of the lower house and to have more chance to concentrate on his special interests. Perhaps there were people he felt he could better help from a position of permanent security.

Throughout his career David Croll's public statements have been remarkably consistent. He supported a budget because it favoured "free competition" and praised the Combines Investigation Act on the ground that it protected the right of consumers to a free choice. As early as 1953 he saw the danger of uncontrolled private television, with its trashy programmes and floods of advertising and said:

> "TV must remain the property of the people and be developed and controlled by them, not by the promoters of breakfast food, soap, cosmetics and patent medicines. No matter how much money they have, it must not be enough."[92]

Only now is the government beginning to guard some of our children, on an experimental basis, against the steady flood of "comedy, quizzes, panel programs, western movies (old and scratchy), and gangster and mystery films with their weird shrieks, pistol shots and bodies falling here and there" which advertisers consider the cheapest way of selling their products.

In the Senate David Croll has continued his fight to protect the consumer. Three times he attempted to secure legislation to compel the credit industry to give the consumer a true picture of what credit buying was actually costing him. At last we are in a reasonably good position to judge various means of financing our purchases.

But the most spectacular of David Croll's senatorial projects has been his chairmanship of the Special Committee on Poverty which held hearings across the country between 1968 and 1971. The report of the special committee is massive, and is confronted with another report called "The Real Poverty Report" signed by four staff members who started their master work by telling Senator Croll to "get stuffed," and who sanctimoniously declared that they could "no longer contribute to a document that was obviously intended to be more useful to politicians than the poor."

I have to confess that I have not ploughed through either publication, though I have read several reviews by people whos prejudices I knew and could allow for. I have also studied in some detail a small publication called "Highlights from the Report of the Special Senate Committee: Poverty in Canada." I don't think I personally agree with either report, although I don't consider myself an expert. I think a lot of welfare work is more self-regarding that other-oriented; we don't like poverty or sickness or physical or mental handicaps because the sight of them makes us uncomfortable.

But David Croll's family were poor when they came to Canada. The families of several of the people who have been most loved and admired among those of whom I have been writing, indeed of those who have apparently been happiest and most successful, have been quite poor. What was the difference between those families and the families that are dirty and ignorant or that sit and stare at the wall with glazed eyes? If we could give everyone the social and spiritual background which shaped the start of John Diefenbaker or Robert McClure or Chief Dan George, that would really be worth doing. But whether a guaranteed annual income would do it or not I don't know.

However, that's not the point. We won't have a true estimate of the value of the poverty study for years. It has made us aware of a problem. It has made us think. Some at least of the practical suggestions will be implemented. But its main interest for me is as an indication of what is going on in the mind of a man who is well past his threescore years and ten, and who has been doing several men's work most of the time. His brain is as keen as ever; his grasp of a complicated situation as comprehensive; his passion for helping people as sincere. He is generous and kindly and when he pauses to talk to you it is like sunshine coming out to warm you on a winter day. Whatever his income he will never be poor because he will always be looking ahead to something he wants to do tomorrow.

Faith

Through the dark shades of convoluted trees,
    Thick with the boskage of embattled night,
Rooted in worn-out wastage of the past,
    We bear our burdens out into the light.

We clear the land and till the ragged field;
    All that we have and are goes to the task;
We would make plain the path for those who come,
    A more abundant life than they could ask.

The grains are clean and golden as we reap,
    Praying the bread of life be ground from these,
And centuries later, over gnarled black roots,
    Our children's children struggle through the trees.

Each of us spins a thread as best he can
    Out of the days and powers he receives;
Only the Weaver, through the circling years,
    Can understand the pattern that He weaves.

But each of us must strongly spend his toil
    Throughout the bitter blindness of the night,
In faith that He Who made us like Himself
    At last will lead us all into His light.

The Healers 14

Universal Donor

This is my blood, shed for you.
See, I give you the transfusion, and finish the operation.
It is nothing. It did not hurt me.
It was the quickest thing I could do.

A doctor must reverence life if he means to save it.
I am a universal donor,[93] and every man is his brother's keeper,
And every man is my brother.

Healing is my gift, but it is useless unless I share it.
I get no satisfaction in sitting at home and hibernating,
Or in being over-fed or entertained or amassing property.
It is a keen delight to conquer disease and suffering;
It is the fullness of life to be able to save a life.

Dr. Robert McClure & Others

If Senator Croll devoted his life to the cause of the weak, the needy and the under-privileged in Canada, and found achievement and satisfaction in doing so, Robert Baird McClure found equal fulfilment as a missionary-surgeon. He did not have to decide to become a missionary; he was born one, in Portland, Oregon, where his mother had been evacuated during the Boxer Riots in China. As soon as possible the family returned to China, where young McClure received his elementary education in mission schools.

He matriculated from Harbord Collegiate, Toronto, in 1917, and received his M.B. in 1922. He had just arranged for two years of public health work at Harvard, when he was asked to step into the shoes of a missionary who had been killed by bandits. By 1923 he was back in China. With a short break for surgical studies in Edinburgh, where he became a Fellow of the Royal College of Surgeons, he spent the next twenty-five years in and around that great country.

He worked in mission hospitals in Honan and Taiwan until war made this impossible. Then he became Field Director for the International Red Cross during the Sino-Japanese War, during which he met Chou-en-lai and Mao-Tse-tung. He told an interviewer for *Maclean's* how he and Dr. Norman Bethune talked with the Chinese Communist leaders about the distribution of Red Cross supplies, which the latter said should go first of all to the fighting men so that the fighting could sooner be brought to an end. It has always been Dr. McClure's contention, however, that political affiliations and considerations make no difference and that aid should be given on the basis of need.

He was not a Communist, and he did not die as Bethune did to become one of their heroes. There were other things for him to do. He remained with the International Red Cross until the end of the war in 1941, giving impartial aid to all in need. And he left as his legacy, not a legend, but the practical scheme for the "bicycle doctor" which he had worked out in the Presbyterian Hospital at Honan.

The need for doctors was so vast and the supply of fully-trained men so completely inadequate that Dr. McClure arranged for the qualified men to train chosen Chinese laymen in basic medicine. These student doctors learned how to lance boils, vaccinate and treat the all too common hookworm. The idea is now being implemented on a large scale, not only in China but in the developing countries.

From 1941 to 1948 we find Dr. McClure on the Burma Road with a Friends' Ambulance Unit, commissioned by the Canadian Red Cross. Here again his services were freely given to all. He must have been quite at a loss during the brief interlude of private surgical practice in Toronto which followed, both as to fees—his salary had heretofore ranged around $3,000 to $5,000 a year—and as to equipment. In the Orient he had performed as many as 1,000 operations a year, ranging from delicate brain surgery to the removal of warts. "He used bicycle spokes to set broken bones, and devised a giant razor blade to slice off skin needed for grafting at a thickness of 1/20,000 of an inch."[94]

Apparently he preferred the harder life for in 1950 he was off again to spend four years with the Anglicans helping Palestinian refugees on the Gaza strip. After that came thirteen or fourteen years in charge of the Ratlam Mission Hospital in Central India, where, amazingly, he spent a term as president of a Rotary Club. He was also vice-president of the Christian Medical Association of India, 1962-65, and Madhya Pradesh Medical Association, 1962-67.

In 1968 Dr. McClure had thoughts of retirement in a neat little bungalow in Toronto. He was of an age to retire, but he wasn't allowed to do so. His fellow churchmen wished to show him respect and they made him Moderator of the General Synod. He was the first layman to have this honour. He received two D.D.'s, a D.Litt.S. and an LL.D. from Universities in Saskatchewan and British Columbia as well as Ontario. He has spoken forthrightly and emphatically about things he knew and felt. And now he has gone to Borneo to work for two years among people who twenty-five years ago were head-hunters, in an eighty-bed jungle hospital, accessible only by motorboat up a tropical river. Since by refusing to accept the moderator's $16,000 salary, which most people would consider modest for the job, Dr. and Mrs. McClure have refrained from accustoming themselves to "affluence", they expect to be "very comfortable."

Dr. McClure does not hesitate to criticize where he feels it is needed. After the Pakistan Civil War, he praised the Canadian government, but thought that private citizens were not giving as much help as they ought. He especially condemned the "hippies" from this continent who had "invaded" India, and lined up at the soup kitchens of the religious institutions. "With all their *guru* stuff", he told the Toronto *Star* in 1971, "they don't know anything about the *Ahimsa,* or life of voluntary poverty and service." To prove your worth, he said, "You don't need money, any more than the man in the moon."[95] But you do need to be useful. He has no respect for spongers. And he has no envy for the prosperous North American business man.

> "He runs himself ragged. If he doesn't necessarily end up in an asylum, he has an awful gnawing inside him of dissatisfaction. Very often he ends up as an alcoholic because of frustration. Or he goes plunging into a hobby or an extra-curricular activity—politics or something like that—and he plunges in so deep that it's abnormal because he's trying to work off this frustration of not being useful.
> "We assume that our way of life is a terrifically fine one, but when you get outside of Canada and look in there are a lot of gaps. There are terrible gaps in family life, the relationship of husband to wife, parent to child. Our relationship to old folks is among the worst in the world."

Canadians are miserly with their churches, Dr. McClure believes. None of us contribute anything like the amount, in proportion to our incomes, that Indians give to their temples, for example. He was never tempted, himself, by the thought of the $100,000 a year he might have made as a surgeon in Canada. People who are supposed to be living in the lap of luxury have never seemed to him to be exceptionally happy.

Nor was the first lay moderator of the United Church much of a theologian in spite of his honorary degrees in divinity and such. He was elected, he told *Maclean's,* because "they wanted a clear view of the relationship of the Canadian citizen to the needs of a very shrinking world." Two or three years earlier, when he was still in India, he had had the opportunity to attend a world conference of medical missionaries in Germany to study the theology of medical missions, and he had refused saying it was "all the bunk." You can take care of a garden without studying botany, and for his purposes he considered a knowledge of orthopedics and leprosy as more vital than any theology. When pressed for a statement of his theological orientation, he offered one which was both simple and profound, and which goes far to explain him:

"My creed has two essential phases. The first is that the God I worship is the God of love, and the second is that the God I worship is the God and Father of all men. And I mean all men, all races, all colours and all religions. Without any distinction whatever. This is the basis of my racial, interracial thinking. It's the philosophy that carried me into medical mission work and sustained me."[96]

Happy is the man who believes in a loving Heavenly Father as his Personal God and Guide, for he is never alone, never discouraged, always looking to the future, and always ready to serve where and how he is needed.

There are many such men in all religions, not only in Christian churches, but in synagogues, mosques and temples. They may not use the same language, but they have opened their hearts to the same Way, and share the peace and confidence it produces. Since this is my personal golden string and I am winding into it those whom I have known or known about personally, and whose words and behaviour have had an impact on me long before I started to put these thoughts together, perhaps I may be forgiven for speaking of one or two more members of my own church whose challenges might seem less arduous than Dr. McClure's, but who were very significant in their very different way.

There are healers of the body, and healers of the mind or soul, Dr. McClure was both. But there are many religious leaders who are just healers of the mind and soul. They also feel their work is important and leave it reluctantly. Clergy, rabbis and other religious leaders often continue, after formal retirement, to serve on the boards of various social welfare, health and educational institutions. Others write newspaper columns and books; they retire on small farms or in country villages, where they can at least have vegetable gardens, a few fruit trees, and perhaps some chickens; some of them even run for public office.

An example of the last category is the Rev. Stewart East of Islington United Church, who was elected to the Etobicoke Council in the same year in which he retired from the active ministry. He repeated, and at the same age, the record of his father, an ardent social reformer who was actually jailed for a short time because of his support of the trek of the unemployed through Regina during the "dirty thirties". Dr. East is still as irrepressible as he was in his twenties.

When I asked him why he was interested in being in council he explained that a cluster of large apartments was going up in the vicinity of his church, which would bring 6,000 new people into the neighbourhood. Too often, when apartments come in, churches die. Apartment dwellers are too often transient, without roots in the community. This is probably one of the seeds of the inner dissatisfaction of which so many of them complain. It certainly hurts the churches. Dr. East hopes to get himself appointed a lay reader in the Anglican church, and to line up all the churches on a completely ecumenical basis to bring the new residents into a close relation with the community. And he believes the easiest meeting-place for old and new residents is in the churches.

But, in the United Church at least, by far the largest group of retired clergymen who are still *un*tired remain as pastoral assistants or supply ministers or chaplains in some institution. That is, they keep on doing pastoral work, because it is their life. Their wives usually share this continuing interest as Amy McClure has shared Dr. McClure's. Such a couple were my friends Lavell and Emily Smith. Lavell died as I was completing this book. I think he died content, and I think I know something of the why and how.

Perhaps I am assuming too much in calling them friends, for I never knew either of them intimately. Emily and I entered Victoria College in the Fall of 1917. I think she was a year or so older than I but we were all of us very young and innocent. The only boys in our year were pretty young too, or delicate, and there were very few of them. Emily lived at home with her father, Dean McLaughlin, and I was in residence, and we were not in the same course, but I thought she was lovely-looking, serene and sweet. I still felt this the last time I saw her, quite recently at a class reunion.

After the war ended, Lavell came back from overseas in the middle of our college years. The boys were now in the majority, but they were not boys: they were men. They were older in years because of the time they had lost, and they were vastly older in experience. Some of them frightened me. But the first impression I had of Lavell was of gentleness and kindness, and when I had a chat with him at one of the receptions,—conversaziones I think we called them then— he didn't make me feel ill at ease. When I heard that he and Emily were married, I thought it was a perfect match.

He took his B.A. in 1921, and his B.D. in New York two years later. He looked after Christian education for three years at West-

123

minster Church on Bloor Street in Toronto, and then spent three and a half in the pastorate in Huntsville, Ontario. After that he became senior minister in Westmount Park United Church in Montreal. It was a big charge for a young man only seven or eight years out of college. He stayed there ten years, and I am told that he and Emily were both very much loved.

Dr. Victor E. Frankl has pointed out that circumstances have very different effects on different people. Even in concentration camps, where so many were reduced to an almost vegetable level and a few became unutterably degraded, some were close to becoming saints. I don't know what Lavell Smith's war experiences were, although I've been told he had a very fine record, but I think it may well have given him the sense of dedication—the "something to look forward to"— that Frankl considers essential to the maintenance of healthy morale. He knew what he had to do in life, and at first, though challenging, it was not too hard.

The hard time came when people saw that a new war was going to be declared. I think anyone who reads the New Testament honestly knows that Jesus was not a believer in war. But most of us so-called Christians believed our case was exceptional. We believed we were in the right. God was on our side. Some of us said with profound after-wisdom that if we had helped the Weimar Republic the Nazis would never have come into power, but that didn't help us when we faced Hitler. Even today we have not learned our lesson and would destroy the world before we would share our affluence with less fortunate nations or even with the underprivileged in our own country. At any rate most people allowed themselves to be whipped into a war fervour. Five or six ministers in the United Church refused to do so. They signed and made public a pacifist manifesto which put them squarely in opposition to the popular position. Among these was the Reverend Lavell Smith. Presently I heard that he had resigned from his church. Everyone said it was inevitable.

At that time I was living in the country, looking after my parents, who were ill. I could have issued all the manifestos I liked and nobody would have taken any notice. So I took A.R.P. training, tried to follow all the regulations, and wrote sad, cynical little poems in private. I couldn't have done anything to stop the war, I told myself; whether my country was right or wrong, if it went down to defeat I didn't want to survive.

Of course the manifesto didn't stop war; all it did was stop what

124

looked like being a brilliant career. Except that sometimes when I was tempted to remain silent I would remember the pacifist manifesto of the United Church ministers and nerve myself to the effort of saying something embarrassing or dangerous. And who can say how many hundreds or even thousands of others did the same?

The next time I encountered the Lavell Smiths they were back in Toronto, at the Church of all Nations. It was a mission charge. They seemed serene and happy, but reluctant to talk of the past. I tried to tell them what their courage had meant to me—for of course Lavell must have talked it over with Emily before he took such a step—foolhardy from a worldly point of view—but they appeared not to think it important. They were very casual about it all.

The Smiths remained with the Church of all Nations until it was time for Lavell to superannuate. The work they must have done in that seventeen years is incalculable. A mission in downtown Toronto ministering to strangers and drawing them into brotherhood, a church trying to help the needy and lonely and under-privileged without turning them into political activists and being more divisive than brotherly—it is certainly the place for a follower of the gospel of peace. I saw the Smiths occasionally while they were there, for Lavell was the permanent president of our college class, and he and Emily always seemed unchanged, a little older perhaps, but always with that radiance. When the time came for retirement from the active work, Lavell continued in connection with Humbercrest Church, first as assistant minister in charge of visiting, and then as pastor emeritus, but still visiting until he was nearly eighty. "He was a tower of strength to all his friends," one of them told me; "full of love and faith."

Until the end he also remained on the board of the Lavell Smith Homes for the Aged, two old houses in the Parkdale area which he acquired when first the housing problem for people on low fixed incomes became acute. The Presbytery helped a little, I am told, but the funds came mostly from private sources. It was Lavell Smith's own project; he sparked it and put it through and helped to keep it going. It is a fitting monument to one who, like Abou ben Adhem, "loved his fellow-men."[97]

Lavell was a saintly person, with the humility which is so important in religious life. He made no demands, uttered no recriminations. In this way he made age a beautiful completion to a beautiful life and death merely the other face of birth.

Light of the World

Who are the happy people?
Are they those who grasp and store
And, whatever goods God sends them,
Are always wanting more?
    No, their brows are knit with worry
    And their mouths are hard and dry,
    While the light on good men's faces
    Is like sunshine in the sky.

Some are avid for excitement,
And the whirligig and din
That fever-flush their faces
Say poison lurks within;
    Faster they whirl and faster,
    Maddened, afraid to cease,
    But the light on good men's faces
    Is the homing light of peace.

There's a spark in wit and beauty
And a glow in power and fame,
But the light on good men's faces
Puts these shallower lights to shame.
    No blasts of failure quench it,
    Nor showers of sorrow damp
    The light on good men's faces
    Where God has lit the lamp.

The Mother   **15**

Motherhood

What will you do with your child,
Mary by the manger?
What will you do with this small sweet
Innocent stranger?
Never again he may
Lie as soft as he lies today;
Smother him in the manger
Under the fragrant hay.

What have you done with your child,
Mary by the altar?
I warned you not to let him live;
Why did you falter?
Why did you make no plea?
What is life if it must be
Offered upon the altar,
Offered upon the tree?

What have you done with your life,
Mary, loving and giving?
When you have lost the meaning of life,
What is the use of living?
Empty are sea and sod
Though time is long and the earth is broad!
"Burdens are part of living;
"My son was the son of God.

"We cannot shape their lives.
"All we can do is pray
"And love and hope that they may find
"The harder, higher way,
"That a man may be a man,
"That a woman do what a woman can,
"That they find the parts they were meant to play
"In God's eternal plan."

Massachusetts, in Uganda, and in London, England. Under the name of Father Benedict, Georges has become a Trappist monk in Oka, bound by a vow of silence. Bernard, a painter, is married and lives abroad. Michel, the youngest, also married but still living in Canada, is a scholar and writer. Jean, the fourth brother, has completed his Ph.D. and established homes for retarded men near Paris, France and in England and Canada and India.

With talent, education and social position behind them, these five young people could have set their sights where they would. Why have all five turned their attention away from the fields in which worldly success is most likely to be obtained? Why, with the possible exception of the author and the artist, have they undertaken lives of endless, and seemingly often wearisome service? Obviously they must have grown up feeling that such a life was a good and satisfying one.

Life had been strenuous for the Vanier family during the second world war. In 1940 they fled from Paris before the German advance. Madame Vanier was evacuated from Bordeaux with other Canadians aboard a Canadian destroyer. Her husband escaped in a sardine boat, and they met again in London where he became official representative to Charles de Gaulle's Committee of National Liberation. In recognition of her work with the St. John Ambulance Voluntary Aid Department during the First World War and her work with the Canadian Red Cross during the Second, Madame Vanier was made Chevalier de la Légion d'Honneur, Dame of the Order of Malta, and Dame of the Order of St. John of Jerusalem. In 1946 she also received the Jacques Cartier medal struck by the French Government to honour Canadians who had given "notable assistance" to France; it recognized her work "for the French people, particularly prisoners of war and displaced persons."

"A woman who entertained French resistance leaders in Algeria during the Second World War and sneaked into France in a stolen Red Cross uniform as the War ended"—a way of putting things that is perhaps more journalistic than realistic—is not going to give up her work for the needy when peace comes, though her aims take on a new colouring. Madame Vanier came back to a Canada entering the age of violence, the age of detachment, of disillusionment, of the generation gap, of drugs and dirt and rock music, of repudiation of the old ways by the young. Her work in "the slums and prisons of Paris and Montreal", according to Gail Scott of Canadian Press[100] convinced her that "the family tradition holds the key to cure the

Mme. Georges-P. Vanier

If there is any aristocracy in Canada it is to be found in Québec. This aristocracy is extremely durable, both among individuals and among families.

In writing of Senator Thérèse Casgrain (née Forget) I have mentioned her and her husband's distinguished ancestors dating back two or three centuries. The Auberts de Gaspé and de la Chesnaye, are a similarly long lived and active stock.[98] The author of *"Les anciens canadiens"* wrote this early Canadian classic at the age of seventy-six in his manor-house after retiring from a strenuous career as high sheriff of the district of Québec; the families are still active. Other early settlers with notable descendants include the Babys, the Berthelots, the de Lérys, the Héberts, and others. But none was more distinguished than that of de Salaberry.

This old, seigneurial family has intermarried with seigneurial families. Its manor-house near Québec city served as headquarters for Montcalm during the Seven Years' War. Afterwards, however, the family rejected the lures of American-type "freedom". They accepted the British connection and aided in the defence of their cit and province against the invading revolutionary armies in 1775. An again during the war of 1812.

Pauline Vanier is a daughter of Justice Charles Archer a Thérèse de Salaberry. She received the education common for I class, in a convent and from private tutors. She entered society a married. Her husband was a soldier. He had a distinguished ca in two world wars, despite the loss of a leg. He spent thirty-five y in the diplomatic service, beginning as an aide to Governor-Ger Byng in 1921, one of the first two Canadians to hold such a post, ending as the first Canadian ambassador to France. Throughou career Madame Vanier was always at her husband's side or w call, "one of those rare women," as Jeannine Locke comment 1966, "whose grace and beauty have increased with age and shared with him an aristocratic devotion to duty and a n indifference to money."[99]

During these years Madame Vanier bore and raised five ch all of whom share their parents' sense of public duty, and all o can stand on their own feet and yet lend a helping hand to The only daughter is a doctor; she has worked in hospitals in anguishes of human existence." And although she worked in other fields this was constantly in her mind and in her discussion with her husband and friends. Her own life bears witness to the sincerity of her convictions and to the truth of her judgement.

For seven and a half years, while her husband was Governor-General, Pauline Vanier accompanied him on the many trips he made to various parts of Canada, hoping to bring the various parts of the country closer to each other. Yet she had time for many and varied benevolent and recreational organizations. She was particularly interested in retarded children and was present at many gatherings called to study their problems or bring them a better life. She was patroness of many national groups including the affiliated May Court Clubs of Canada, the Hadassah-Wizo Ottawa Council and others. She received eight honorary degrees during those years, and was deeply interested in education and social science. She and her husband held an annual Christmas party for the Ottawa Boys' Club.

By 1964 Their Excellencies had decided they would like to see established in their native land "an enduring association of many professions dedicated to the reinforcement of family living."[101] With this in mind they invited prominent sociologists, social workers, scholars and religious leaders to a Conference on the Family. At this conference General Vanier said in part, on behalf of both himself and his wife:

> "Canada has a prodigious heritage, We can and must move forward to our true destiny as a country opposed to pure materialism.
>
> "Let us find once more the flame that lit the way for the first missionaries and pioneers.
>
> "The amazing development of economic and material civilization has brought a crisis upon the family. It is time for men with serious responsibilities in society to take stock together of the problem facing us. . . . The problem is in our hands. It is up to us to direct the course of civilization."[102]

At the conference, as noted in the sketch on Dr. Wilder Penfield, it was decided to set up a permanent organization which should be called the Vanier Institute of the Family. Dr. Wilder Penfield accepted the presidency. The Governor-General and Madame Vanier became honorary patrons. General Vanier finalized his introduction to Dr. Penfield's little book on the Family and the Institute on his death-bed breathing oxygen, and signed it on the day before he died.

Madame Vanier never sought public recognition for her social service; she wished it all to be regarded as a part of her husband's work. Even now it is not easy to get specific facts, though all accounts stress the large part it played in her life. In spite of her reticence she became widely known and was named Canadian Woman of the Year in 1965.

In 1966, the year before her husband's death, she opened the Mme. Vanier Children's Services Treatment Centre in Ottawa. Earlier in that same year she had become the first lay chancellor of the University of Ottawa. In her inaugural address she spoke of the "ideal of justice and mutual understanding between our two founding peoples" which lay behind the "fraternal co-existence" of the university. She spoke of the principles which are the "essence and foundation of our western civilization," and of the faith which "far from being outmoded and old-fashioned, imparts a beauty, a richness and radiance that can be found in no other source." During her remarks her husband, also on the platform, never took his eyes off her.

Other honours for Madame Vanier followed her husband's death. She became a Companion of the Order of Canada, a director of the Bell Telephone Company and the Bank of Montreal, a director of the Montreal Institute of Cardiology, and a member of the Privy Council. In 1967 she won the Cardinal Newman award, given annually to a member of the Roman Catholic laity who has made a notable contribution to the country's intellectual life and has exemplified Christian principles in public activities. In 1968 she was cited by the Montreal Citizenship Council for her efforts to promote good citizenship, and she chaired the National Conference on Poverty at the University of Montreal.

But Pauline Vanier had never wanted power or glory. She admits that she is old-fashioned, but she feels that unless a mother *must* be out of her home working, and her children know she has to be, she is robbing them of part of the love and security they need. The mother who is bored with housework and wants "a life of her own", may well lose her greatest asset. By trying to be like men women lose their sensitivity, their intuition. If they enter politics it should be for a cause in which they believe, and because they have something to contribute, but not merely to compete for power. I don't think she would want to see even the men doing that and she has

132

evidently created a home atmosphere in which her children all grew up with higher goals. She has shown that wifehood and motherhood can be a sustained and satisfying career, preserving some of the dearest values of our race.

And now she has gone from us, to be in France, nearer to her children, and above all nearer to Jean, and to his work with handicapped people. Jean Vanier believes that the world has never been on such a brink of disaster, with revolution, famine and war. The old approach to welfare is no longer enough. It cannot be left to the professionals, or to the odd moments a volunteer can spare from a busy life. It involves the gift of oneself. "I am only selling a few luxuries I don't need, with the permission of my children," says Madame Vanier, "and using the money to help the poor in general and my son's work in France, England, Canada and India." She may come back; she is keeping her home and furniture. But I think she will not. She has responded to a great need with a mother-heart that has never considered any other task in life half so important as being a good mother. A second career at seventy-three? No, an expansion of her life. After all, as she says herself, it is a great responsibility to be the mother of Jean Vanier.

Compensation

> Weep not, lady growing old
>   For lark and morning light;
> Sing within the heart of age
>   The nightingales of night,
> Soar less high in blue above
> But know far more of pain and love.
>
> Mourn not, wise man, man of strength,
>   If you reach no goal;
> Through the untiring effort you
>   Will find that you are whole
> And surrender comes to be
> That which heals and sets you free.

The Wise Man 16

Prayer of the Son of Earth

Manitou, mighty Spirit,
    I lift my face to the sun;
Give me eyes like the eagle's,
    Deer-speed to run.

May I learn the wolf's wild courage,
    And, like the bear, be strong;
Teach me the serpent's cunning
    And the bird's song.

Teach me the water's laughter,
    The sudden bright release
Of sunrise and of springtime
    And evening peace.

This is your earth that stretches
    Far as a man can see.
Make me know I am part of it
    And it is part of me.

Chief Dan George

I sometimes think our so-called "western civilization" is the only one which despises age. Perhaps that is putting it too cruelly. Perhaps it is just our hurry, our eagerness for change. But when I hear "Chinese ancestor-worship" treated as if it were a childish superstition, I wonder if people really believe in any survival after death. If they did would they not expect the protection of strong and loving spirits to continue. And when Harold Cardinal of the Alberta Crees talks to me in his thoughtful musical voice about what the "old men" think, there is a respect in his tones that convinces me he considers them wise men as well. If they have lived well, that is what they should be, and perhaps it is better to call them that. More precisely, I use that term when I talk about the quality which I feel in Chief Dan George.

There has been a lot of discontent among Indians in Canada, and Harold Cardinal has been a part of it. He has been a leader among the young people of his race, and has presented their demands strongly and sometimes angrily. I am glad if he is beginning to listen to the old men, who are generally more patient. Social changes do not come about overnight, even if all thinking people want them. And when people are divided as they are—including the Indian people themselves—it is very hard to follow a strong course towards change.

In 1969, after a couple of decades of grants and subsidies to the Indian peoples of Canada and to the organizations they set up, the Federal Government presented a white paper, suggesting, among other reforms, abolition of the Indian Affairs branch, and ownership of reserve land by Indians with complete freedom to maintain, use or alienate. The paper suggested complete integration of the Indian and white communities as far as education, health and other provincial services are concerned, with of course, a corresponding liability on the part of the Indians to pay taxes. This was indignantly repudiated by the Indians, particularly by Mr. Cardinal, author of "The Unjust Society",[103] in "Citizens Plus", often known as the Red Paper. The British Columbia Indians, the longest and possibly the best organized, offered still a third policy statement. "The Brown Paper."

To one who had always admired the Indian people and had sought long and earnestly for an Indian graft in her own family tree, all this

135

was very confusing and sad. It was a really thrilling experience to hear Chief Dan George speak to a dinner of the Canadian Council of Christians and Jews and lift the whole problem onto a higher plane. Everything I have read of him since has confirmed me in the feeling that he has learned to live and will not be disturbed, though saddened by the wrangling.

His Indian name (or one of his names, because he has different names in the different tribes in which he has been asked to serve as honorary chief) is Nan-wah-nath. It may be roughly translated as "He who goes round giving the shirt off his back to any one who needs it without seeking any return." He is poor because as soon as he gets anything, someone wants to borrow it, and he seems unable to resist. Anyone who is hungry or without a roof over his head can come to him. In fact, although he was the hereditary chief of the Salish tribe he surrendered the title to his brother, bringing him back for the purpose from the United States where he had had the bad luck of the "Prodigal Son."

For years Dan was a logger on the reserve and later a longshoreman. Then he was badly injured when his whole body was crushed by a load of timber and his active career was at an end. It is a pity he was not on the docks early enough to work with J. S. Woodsworth, the former Methodist minister who broke with the church over its acceptance of the popular policies on labour and war. Perhaps he did know the older man slightly; in many ways the desire of Chief Dan George for peaceful settlement of disputes reminds me of Mr. Woodsworth's.

The family, who were devoted to each other, spent a number of years also on the fair circuit, doing the rodeos and square dance parties. Then Bob, the eldest, became a star in Paul St. Pierre's Caribou series, which ran for three years. Eventually it was bought by the Walt Disney Productions.

It was through Bob that Dan got his first chance to act. One of the chaps who was supposed to play in "Smith", was no longer available, and they couldn't find a replacement. Bob asked if an Indian wouldn't do. Dan was tried out and fitted in.

In 1969 Gene Lasko, associate producer of "Little Big Man", saw what he called a "remarkable" face on a still outside a small theatre where "Smith" was playing. It was the only moving picture in which seventy-one-year-old Dan had even appeared. But they had tried in vain for Sir Laurence Olivier and other distinguished actors;

perhaps they could do with somebody who looked as if he actually were the character.

They found the Chief on the Burrard Reserve near North Vancouver, not anxious to act, since he thought Western stories and pictures always misrepresented the Indians. He thinks "Little Big Man" is different; you can see that Custer really got what he deserved. And in any case the relationship of the white boy and his Indian grandfather shows the worth of integration. "And that's what I've dedicated my life to."[104]

Chief Dan would like to change the public image of the Indian through history, and thus rebuild Indian morale. He tells us that the Indians are essentially a gentle people, with a deep love for nature, from which they only took what they needed, and that with apologies and thanks. He can remember his father intoning his prayer of thanksgiving to the sunrise as it lit fires on the peak of Mount Pay-nay-nay. He knew his people when there was still dignity in their lives, "unspoken confidence in the home and a certain knowledge of the path we walked upon." He does not blame the white man for the lack of moorings of his people, the ugly surroundings when beauty is so necessary, the ridicule, the pity, the sneers. He does ask us to imagine what it is like to be belittled, to be left without pride in your race, your family, yourself.

You don't care about tomorrow, for what does tomorrow matter. You get drunk for a few brief moments to escape from ugly reality and feel important, and when you wake next morning it is worse, for the alcohol did not really fill the emptiness but only dug it deeper.

The potlatch, which was a feast with gifts, was part of the old religion, and giving has usually been as important to the Indian as receiving. Now when the white man suggests integration, says Chief George,

> How can I come? I am naked and ashamed. How can I come in dignity? I have no presents . . . I have no gifts. What is there in my culture you value . . . my poor treasure you can only scorn. . . . I must wait until you want something of me . . . until you need something that is me . . . then I can hold my head high for I will meet you as an equal. . . . We want first of all to be respected and to feel we are people of worth. We want an equal opportunity to succeed in life . . . but we cannot succeed on your terms. . . . We need specialized help

137

... we are people with special rights guaranteed to us by promises and treaties . . . we do not thank you for them because we paid for them. . . . We paid for them with our culture, our dignity, and self-respect. We paid and paid and paid until we became a beaten race, poverty-stricken and conquered."[105] "The only thing that can truly help us is genuine love. You must truly love us, be patient with us and share with us. And we must love you with a genuine love, love which forgives and forgets, a love that forgives the terrible sufferings your culture brought when it swept over like a wave crashing along a beach . . . with a love that forgets and lifts up its head and sees in your eyes an answering love of trust and acceptance."[106]

Here is someone else—someone who has been excluded, patronized, discriminated against—saying the same thing Jean Vanier and his mother say about love, but from the other side of the fence. He also speaks of acceptance. He has this wisdom to offer us. And he also has the old wisdom of his people who loved the earth.

"It is hard for me to understand a culture that not only hates and fights its brothers but even attacks nature and abuses her. I see my white brother blotting out nature from his cities. I see him strip the hills bare, leaving ugly wounds on the faces of mountains. I see him tearing things from the bosom of the earth as though she were a monster who refused to share her treasures with him. I see him throw poison in her waters, indifferent to the life he kills there. And he chokes the air with deadly fumes."[107]

He does not like life in New York. He thinks it's not a good place to live because you have to look up to see the sky. Many more sophisticated people without his background are expressing similar opinions. Many young people are devoting themselves to spreading the same gospel.

But there's something about gentle speech from a man of seventy-three, with muscles like whipcord, and nearing the end of a life of hardship, that is impressive. He carries weight. And I sincerely believe that he carries also sincerity and simplicity and that he speaks from the heart. There is a "wisdom older than walking men" and Chief Dan George has it.

138

Indian Summer

Some men approach their "Indian summer" years
With tense and bitter mouths, with angry fists
And hearts untimely frozen. Some old wound
Still rankles. Some misunderstanding gnaws
Them, as an old dog gnaws a worthless bone
He cherishes to show he still has teeth.

At the flood tide of youth, at manhood's peak,
At the full ripeness of our womanhood,
We could tear down the unconquerable stars
To make a chaplet for someone we love,
Or seize the terrible lightning in our hands
To slash destruction on our enemies.

We shout down opposition, for we know
That we are right. Our way of life is best,
And differing others are unjustified
Completely.
            If they triumph, it is wrong
Prevailing over what it should not dare
To raise its eyes to or, much less, to touch.

But when we have grown old, we should have learned
Issues are shadowy, neither black nor white,
But grey, and there are more important things
In life than legal wrangles, social feuds,
Or even justice. Mercy matters more.

We should have learned to taste the ripening fruit
Of human tolerance and kindliness
Like some sweet Indian summer in our hearts,
To look on all with the benevolent eye
Of autumn suns, to inhale the fragrant air
And share it gladly with whoever comes.

            War comes from lack of human understanding
            That this is not the way to settle problems
            Although it is the way with weeds and flowers

139

Or among animals. It is not even
The way to right a wrong. It comes from fear,
If our high-diked defences yield a crumb,
All that we value will be swept away.
And so we fight, and it is swept away
Even more dreadfully by us ourselves,
Since, fighting, we become that which we fight.
Opponents said to J. S. Woodsworth once
(The noted pacifist), "We must fight fire
With fire," but, smiling gently, he replied
"Fight fire with water, rage with peace, and hate
With patient understanding and with strong
Persistent loving and with tireless faith."
Then Indian summer may come back to us
Before we have destroyed our planet Earth.

The Interpreter 17

Mystery

All sunshine, warmth and sweet delight
The wind has whistled down the night,
Leaving to me distraught and lost,
Only the darkness and the frost.

The frost shall chill and barb my knife
To probe the festering sores of life,
To stir the sleepy-eyed desire
And spark the farthest stars to fire.

The darkness shall be deep with wonder
For all life's secrets buried under,
And out of it my love shall weave
A cloak of peace for those who grieve.

First published in "The New Outlook"

Hugh MacLennan

If I were picking one epithet to attach to the name of Hugh Mac-Lennan, it would not be one of his degrees or honours; I would simply say Hugh MacLennan, Canadian. All the people I have been thinking about are Canadians, and in many ways are typical of some of our best qualities and accomplishments. But they are men and women who have found fairly simple solutions to the problems of today, though by no means easy ones. In many ways they are like scientists who have made valuable discoveries because they have been able to focus their attention on a particular problem and isolate it from others. Hugh MacLennan cannot do this. He is intensely aware of all the problems, and of the facets they present to various people, and of the partial solutions which each offers. His problems are the problems of his country, and they are too complex to be solved by any one man. Our task is rather one of acceptance than of solution.

Professor MacLennan is young yet by my standards. He was born only in 1907. But he is old enough for retirement in this age when the young push the old out so soon into what is for many a prison of useless loneliness. It will never be so for Hugh MacLennan. He has a life in his mind, and a power to share his thoughts with others that should take him well past the three score and ten and perhaps well past the fourscore with the contentment that comes of a full life. There will not be a second career for him, but the opportunity to spend his full time on what I am sure has always been his major interest: his biographies in the various Who's Who type collections defiantly place "Author" or "Writer" ahead of the more secure-sounding Associate Professorship at McGill. As long as he lives, I don't think he will stop writing any more than he can stop thinking. In any case he has at least one more book to write: a third approach to the problem his people failed to solve in "Each Man's Son" and again in "The Return of the Sphinx".

No-one can really fathom the deep wells from which a great author draws his inspiration. His personal experience. His observations, unusually acute and sensitive. His own reflections, profound and searching. We have only the bare facts, the skeleton of his career, together with any conclusions to be drawn from his writing.

Hugh MacLennan was born in Cape Breton island, a coal-mining district of Nova Scotia, with many Scottish families, and much hardship and strong loyalties. His father was a doctor, and served overseas during the First World War, invalided home when he was only nine. According to Hugh's reminiscences in "An Orange from Portugal",[109] he and his mother had been staying with a grandmother in Cape Breton, but went to Halifax to find a house and make it ready for the father's return. This home was wrecked the very day they moved in by their "own private explosion" (not the famous one for which they "had to wait another year"). They transferred to an old residential hotel on Barrington Street until after Christmas, where their meals were brought up to them from the basement kitchen by a boy who is the central character in the story. The boy's mother always wanted rum when she was "feelin' bad". The father, whom the boy idolized, had said that if you wanted "to be a seaman you got to wash out your insides with rum every day." That same father had refused to buy the boy an orange on the ground that if you bought "stuff at the stores" you couldn't go on being a seaman. Anyway store oranges weren't "real."

With amazing sensitivity young Hugh entered into the feelings of this boy, whose father was on a slow convoy in those days when crossing the Atlantic was a chancy business. The father had said that the only "real" oranges were those you picked off the trees in Portugal, and a quaint old lady, also living in the hotel, had convinced the boy that Santa Claus would bring him a "real" orange to show that his father was thinking about him. Hugh had his doubts about the powers of Santa Claus, instilled into him at school and not yet communicated to his parents. He was consumed with anxiety. The more exited the boy got, the more Hugh worried. At last, on Christmas Eve after his own father was snoring, Hugh tried, unsuccessfully, to convoy the orange he found in the toe of his own stocking to Chester's in the basement. He was frustrated by tiny old Mrs. Urquhart, who was also wandering about the halls, fully dressed, and wearing her white lace cap, in the small hours of the morning. Yet when the breakfast tray arrived, Chester showed them a "real" orange, "printed daintly with someone's pen" with the words, *"Produce of Portugal."*

A child so uncomfortably aware of the hopes and possible disappointment of another child, and one he had known only for a few weeks, might have been expected to be permanently damaged by "the famous Halifax explosion" a year later. Instead, it became the core of his first highly successful novel, "Barometer Rising" in 1941, a Book Society Choice and a Book-of-the-Month Club Recommendation. In the mean time he had matriculated at the Halifax Academy, received his B.A. from Dalhousie, his M.A. from Oxford (as a Rhodes Scholar), and his Ph.D. from Princeton, N.J. It was while he was engaged in post-graduate work apparently, that he became conscious in a new way of his Canadianism and of what it meant to be Canadian.

MacLennan tells us the story himself in his essay "On Discovering Who We Are".[110] When he first came home from Oxford in 1932, he applied for a post in the English department at Dalhousie, where there was a vacancy. He was told that he was unlikely to get it, for an Englishman had applied, with the same grades as his own, but— an Englishman. The head of the department recommended he go to "the States"; "A Canadian can always get a job there." When he got home the young Oxford graduate wrote to "every college and university in Canada". The only one with a vacancy in those depression days was a western one, which had two applications from Englishmen and gave him the same advice as the head of the English Department in Dalhousie. Hugh MacLennan took the advice and accepted a fellowship in Princeton. But he did not forget the sentence: "After all, you're a Canadian and he's an Englishman." It had gone from his brain right through him till he "felt it in the back of his legs". And while he was in the United States he found out what it meant to be a Canadian.

He came back to teach in Lower Canada College in Montreal, where he wrote "Barometer Rising" and the first part of "Two Solitudes". A Guggenheim Fellowship then allowed him to leave teaching for a time and devote himself entirely to writing. "Two Solitudes" won the Governor-General's Award for Fiction in 1945; "The Precipice" received the same award in 1948; and "The Watch That Ends the Night" in 1959. He has also written "Each Man's Son", "The Return of the Sphinx", and several volumes of non-fiction. He has accumulated several honorary degrees D.Litt. (6 times), LL.D. (5 times), D.C.L., F.R.S.C. He was awarded the Lorne Pierce Gold Medal for literature in 1952, became a Companion of the Order of Canada in Centennial Year, and is, or has been until recently, on the English staff at McGill University

It sounds like an extremely successful career. Of one thing I am certain, however. No man can write as he does of the struggle of men and women to find themselves and to reach others if he has not himself experienced the terrible aloneness which must come sooner or later to all people with a capacity for clarity of thought, objectivity of judgement, and the imagination which one of our poets has called "the greatest instrument of moral good."[111]

This is no more a book of literary appreciations than a collection of capsule biographies. It is my own compressed search for what enables men and women, particularly man and women of my own age, to come to terms with themselves, those around them, their world, and the Infinite Power of which all these are but mirror fragments. Because of this, I propose to give, as briefly as I can, and as a result of course quite inadequately, some idea of what several of the MacLennan novels have to contribute to this effort. If what I got out of them was not what the author intended, I am still grateful to him.

The theme of "Two Solitudes" appears to be that people and groups move in straitjackets of their inherited and acquired fears, prejudices, resentments, vanities and prides. Their attempts to communicate, to reach each other, are frustrated by their own artificial defences. They are like "thin gnat voices calling from star to star". The best that can be hoped is suggested by the lines from Rainer Maria Rilke from which the book takes its title: "Love consists in this, that two solitudes protect and touch and greet each other."

The first two parts are the tragedy of Athanase Tallard, a free thinker in religion, anxious to work with English-speaking Canadians because he felt that only so could his people gain the hard progress that, like MacLennan, he believed had filtered into the English from the United States. Huntly McQueen, apotheosis of the steel materialism which now seemed the road to prestige and power, planned to build a factory in Tallard's village, but Tallard, like his province, wanted prestige and power without change. Life was complicated by Marius, son of Tallard's saintly first wife, who hated his Irish stepmother, was uncompromisingly anti-English, spoke provocatively at left-wing meetings, often against conscription, and eventually got into a fight with a soldier and injured him seriously. After he fled from the police, and was finally captured, his father quarrelled with the parish priest and was banished from the church. His servants left him, he moved into Montreal, sent his younger son Paul to an English private school, and affiliated himself with the Presbyterian Church to which many of the richest men in Montreal belonged. Ironically, six months after the armistice was signed, Marius, still in the army, was made a lance-corporal. Meanwhile Huntly McQueen got rid of Athanase, now a liability instead of an asset, instead working through the bishop, who was worried about the debt on the village church, and wanted a substantial contribution. Tallard had tried to bring the two solitudes together and had estranged both. On his deathbed he was reconciled to the Church, roused somehow from what seemed to be coma to make confession to his old friend Father Arnaud, and received extreme unction. It is interesting to note that the materialism which MacLennan elswhere associates with puritanism, is associated here with atheism and opposed by parochialism. In the end the old man recovered his sense of belonging through reconciliation to the church of his childhood.

The third and fourth books are primarily the story of Paul, the younger boy, who had been both Protestant and Catholic, both French and English. The life of his older brother Marius was already fixed in a pattern of resistance, and Tallard's widow, a warm, indolent, man's woman, married an American and disappeared from the scene. Paul's life had already become closely interwoven with that of John Yardley, a retired seacaptain from Nova Scotia, who had bought land in the village and become a friend of his father. Yardley's daughter had married into an old Montreal family with considerable wealth and prestige, and she and her elder daughter also moved in the straitjackets of their class. But Yardley took life as he found it and made a warm place for himself in the village; he didn't worry about what people thought of him; he had no pretence and no false pride; he chattered away in his bad French and people liked him because he didn't set up any artificial barriers to prevent them from doing so. His younger granddaughter fell in love with Paul Tallard, and the main theme of the second half of the book is their attempt to find themselves and each other.

At one point MacLennan makes Paul say:

> "Science and war—and God knows what else—have uprooted us and the whole world is roaming. Its mind is roaming, Heather. Its mind is going mad trying to find a new place to live . . . I feel it—right here in myself. I've been living in the waiting room of a railway station."[112]

Paul and Heather left Montreal "to escape the straitjacket of their backgrounds," she to New York to paint, he to a job on a freighter that took him to Athens and eventually led him to Oxford.

His daughter's opposition to the love of Paul and his granddaughter when they finally met again in Halifax was terrible to John Yardley. "In the case of Athanase there had at least been a reason; the legend of a whole race had been against him."[113] It was unbearable that it should affect these two who themselves seemed as open as he in mind and heart.

Yardley was now very old. He had been nearly sixty when he moved to Tallard's village in 1917, and it was now 1939. But his last years had been his best. "There was no limit to what a man could obtain out of life if he merely accepted what lay all around him." But he needed knowledge. Since he had come back to Halifax he had been allowed the use of the Dalhousie library, and had discovered the beauty of art and science. Wonder was around him everywhere. He had been allowed to use the telescope and the microscope. He saw that there was

> "life everywhere and in all things, and in such infinite mani-festations that the brain reeled unless the harmony of the whole entered the mind to reconcile you to your own igno-rance and to beautify the pattern in which you yourself were a part."[114]

Yardley dies, and Marius continues to bind his particular straitjacket of separatism tighter and tighter about himself, but in the end there seems to be hope for Heather and Paul, the young ones.

For MacLennan, it seems to me, the real protagonist in the end turns out to be Canada, where "Night-workers, . . . relaxed and easy with each other, French and English together" share a coffee break in apparent amity, and "even as the two race-legends woke again remembering ancient enmities," the country "took the first irrevocable steps towards becoming herself."

This book was published in 1945. "The Return of the Sphinx", which attacks the same French-English cleavage, came in 1967. Meanwhile came other works in which the canvas is less crowded and the problems more personal.

Most critics see "The Precipice" as the simple struggle of the puritan conscience with the materialistic world it has created and cannot enjoy. There are all sorts of additional sidelights on contem-porary life and problems: Bratian's attribution of the war effort to the herd instinct, and his cynical remark, "If you can make them believe they're fighting for a better world, you can make them believe anything"; Abel Lassiter's comments on fear and how it can be used to gain power; the discussions between Jane and Lucy on cruelty and kindness and lies and truth; the discussions at Bratian's cocktail party; "the gay desperation which made Marcia so vulnerable." Puritanism alone could not explain the nervous restlessness of Stephen Lassiter, contrasting with Lucy's desire for stability and contentment; there is a contrast in this book between the Canadian and American philosophies of life that is always flickering tenuously below the surface, and express itself in Jane's instant reaction to the news of Hiroshima: "The Americans were bound to do something like that one day." And when Stephen faces up to the mess he has made of life he might be quoting from "Death of a Salesman" when he wonders about his children:

> "Would they find anyone to tell them that wanting to be liked, wanting to be admired for doing a good job, was so much too little in this world?"

Life is too complicated to be viewed in terms of one problem, and MacLennan's books are equally rich. He is startling in his insights.

"Each Man's Son" is a tragedy of love and pride, of the attempt to substitute education or physical prowess for love, while separated by pride from those whom we want to love. It is the story of the boyhood of Alan Ainslie, a character of particular significance to MacLennan, since he re-appears as a distinguished politician in "The Return of the Sphinx." His father is an ignorant Scottish prize-fighter, from Cape Breton, who is exploited and destroyed by American and French-Canadian promoters, and returns home to find his wife, after four years of lonely fidelity, on the verge of eloping with another man. She has been driven to this by her love for her son, whom she believes the lonely and self-hating Dr. Ainslie to have been trying to alienate from her with a view to adopting him. McNeil kills both his wife and her lover. The boy is adoptable then, of course, but at the end of the book he is still terrified of the doctor.

"The Return of the Sphinx" again deals with the problems of communication between linguistic groups and generations, but it is also reminiscent of Greek tragedy. Alan Ainslie's son, Daniel, named after Alan's adoptive father, looks and in some ways acts like Alan's real father. In the end he destroys Alan's political career by becoming involved in riots and bombing as suicidally as Archy McNeil plunged into the murder of his wife. Alan Ainslie has been inveigled into politics because he "has a curious mystique about the country," and hopes to unite it. At the end of the book, when the son seems to have destroyed the father, Ainslie says regretfully: "one more step would have freed us all, but the sphinx returned." Then he remembers that this has happened before and man has survived. He still has this vast land, "too vast even for fools to ruin all of it." Life is good and he is grateful to have had a share in it.

> "Looking over the lake he at last accepted that he had merely happened into all this . . . into this loveliness that nobody could understand or possess, and that some tried to control or destroy just because they were unable to possess or understand it. Merely happened into this joy and pain and movement of limbs, of hope, fear, shame and the rest of it, the little chipmunk triumphs and defeats. He believed it would endure. He thanked God that he had been in it, was of it."

MacLennan sees human relations as a central problem in Canada's effort to find herself. Yet the establishment of these is the hardest thing in life.

There is much talk of straitjackets, which prevent people from reaching out naturally to each other. And the solitudes seem to continue to bring pain and destruction. The problems of communication between French-speaking and English-speaking compatriots, between the worshippers of brain and the worshippers of brawn, between urban and rural folk, between men and women and between generations, are all probed gently and understandingly by this great novelist. And in the process he becomes the interpreter of time and eternity and life and death.

In Chapter XI of Part VI of "The Watch That Ends the Night", for example, he is very specific about the relative nature of time. The teller of the story is married to a lovely and loving woman with a great zest for life but with a rheumatic heart that keeps death an ever-imminent reality to them both. And yet during her last months a new element of spiritual communication enters their relationship that makes time itself seem a negligible quantity.

Throughout the book he and his friend, who also had loved Kate and been married to her briefly, are looking for something larger than themselves, to which they must surrender, Jerome laments "God was so convenient for that purpose when people could believe in Him," and thinks they might instead believe in people. For a while

George thinks he might believe in Canada, but in the end it came to him that

> "to be able to love the mystery surrounding us is the final and only sanction of human existence. . . . All our lives we had wanted to belong to something larger than ourselves. We belonged to nothing now except to the pattern of our lives and fates. To God, possibly. I am chary of using that much-misused word, but I say honestly that at least I was conscious of His power."

It has been pointed out that MacLennan blames our puritan background for much of our unhappiness. Of course English Canada shares this with French Canada, for there is much Puritanism in the Catholic Church in Québec, but it is only of English Canada and the United States that MacLennan is speaking in "Cross Country" when he says:

> "America's crisis, and therefore the crisis of the rest of us, consists in this: puritanism has conditioned its members to act rather than to think, to deal with means rather than with ends, to press forward with ever-increasing speed and efficiency toward a material goal."[115]

Again in the prologue to "The Precipice" he remainds us that "Time is more than now, more than twelve o'clock or any particular century. It is also ourselves." And he asks:

> "How near are you then to the end of the journey which the puritans began more than three hundred years ago when they lost hope in themselves and decided to bet their lives on the things they could make rather than on the men they were?"

It is not in these general statements about time and human solitude and the search for human significance, of course, that Hugh Mac-Lennan interprets us to ourselves. To many of us his philosophic statements are difficult, although to those who think in such terms all his work is profoundly suggestive. But the people are Canadian people, their lives conditioned by our terrain, our climate, our history, and our conflicting traditions complicated by our various languages. Canadians are not alone in their anguished reaching out for love and understanding, but they have their own responses, and some of them, I think, might well have an international validity if we could have courage to apply them.

150

The consciousness that life is good, that even a little of it is worth having and enjoying to the full, runs through all Hugh MacLennan's work. Misunderstandings and estrangements are superficial. Loyalties are deep-seated. We must take people as they are and life as it comes and death when we meet it. We can make all beautiful through courage and faith and tenderness. Self-surrender is self-realization. There is always a tomorrow for someone, a tomorrow which we can have helped to build.

Interpenetration

Rich, narrow homeland, clinging to the rim of the wilderness,
Hewn from the forest, miracle of sweet and sudden spring,
Ice break-up, wild geese homing, sap rising in the sugar maple, —
Canada is the bite of an axe, the lift of an untamed wing.

A fire of flowers on the prairie, silver and gold for winning,
A northern lake, a clean-lined ship, a salmon spear,
Masted mountains, a ribbon of rail, solitary elevators, —
Canada is the toil of a beaver, the vision of a mountaineer.

Shadows on the wheatland, shadows on the pasture and orchard,
        autumn
Frost-flavoured, the greedy furnace, the ice-bridge, the hydro ban, —
Canada is a clear-eyed farmer bringing out food for the nations,
A half-frozen Mountie triumphantly bringing in his man.

Planted in defiance of climate and economic and political geography,
By losers, and built in fear and compromise, our country has grown
Stronger with each failure, crisis and impossibility surmounted,
Beautiful, valiant, patient, resolute, and our own.

The
Gate

Co-Operation

Not when grippers and conveyors snarl behind you,
    Rabidly snatching at your hurried hands;
Not when the wheels spin faster, faster, and blind you,
    Whirling as dizzily as the prairie sands;

        Not where explosion suddenly crashes to disaster
            And slow despair drips bloodily between
        The cogs, can man see beauty in his master,
            The inexorably adequate machine.

Deep in the multifarious, fierce connection
    Of every smallest part to serve the whole,
I see the clear, smooth-running, strong perfection
    Of some complex, co-ordinated goal

        When men, in mutual service comprehending
            Their mutual comradeship, shall learn to feel
        Brotherhood, all-embracing and unending,
            Last, loveliest wonder of the age of steel.

And So

We come to the end of our quest.

Canada is our Jerusalem. Here if anywhere, we must find heaven's gate. And no human creature can find heaven's gate in any country unless he loves it as a man loves his mother and a mother loves her child. That is why it is right when we make our living in a country for us to become citizens there. Only so can we repay the land for what it has given us, and only so can we find fulfilment in its open arms.

Canada is not perfect. It is a young country and a rich country, perhaps too rich for its youth. But it is a modest country too, and a tolerant one. Talk about our having no colourful characters in Canada—why the country is full of them—that's why none of them stand out as they do in countries more conventional and more controlled. I could have named hundreds just around me, and thousands, probably, if I had had time and money to cross Canada and look up old friends. Not all are as well known as those I have spoken of here; some of them not known at all outside a little circle. But they are vital and useful.

There is a durability about the typical Canadian. He has to be durable to live in this huge stormy-weathered country with its extremes of heat and cold, its social and economic problems, its diverse cultures all lustily shouting for recognition.

We have talked about the search for knowledge and understanding, which together lead us to the truth. We have talked about the desire for achievement, within an understanding of our own powers and opportunities. First among the men and women of power, who have changed the face of our country, but also among the men and women whose achievements have been directed to a particular field of excellence. And we have talked about the search for life's meaning, and the qualities and motivations which enable people to live on, not in labour and weakness, but well and happily, long past the age of three score and ten and even the age of four score or four score and ten.

First of all assets for this I would place curiosity. It is a characteristic of all the higher animals, but overwhelmingly greater in man. It is the basis of scientific research, travel, and much reading. It can even take the simple form it took with my aunt, who had her kitchen at the front of the house with a lunch bar below a big picture window and could report to me daily on what every living creature in the neighbourhood had done all day long. She was crippled with arthritis, but she took a vicarious pleasure, a little shocked perhaps, because of the slacks, when the young creature across the road was on top of the roof with her husband, helping him to shingle the new bungalow. Or there is the retired librarian whom I met for the first time in the Interrogative Club in the autumn of 1917, hampered even then with an amputation, but still getting around today and still living a rich full life with her books.

It's splendid, as you grow older, to have something interesting to do, or alternatively to be able to be interested in what you have to do. And it's good to have it carry over so that there is always something to look forward to. Wordsworth talks about how a child

> "more than all other gifts
> That earth can offer to declining man,
> Brings hope with it, and forward-looking thoughts
> And stirrings of inquietude, when these
> By tendency of nature needs must fail."[116]

Those "stirrings of inquietude" might be interpreted less rosily than in Wordsworth's lines if some grandparents were consulted about their function as baby-sitters, but a great deal of pleasure can come from such contacts. Teddy Bywater looks forward to being the oldest man at the Dominion Day celebrations in East York every year and Mrs. Pennells looks forward to playing at the annual recreation dinner and similar affairs.

There are many who crave more direct and continuous action, and want to feel that they are still having some sort of full-time participation in society. They continue to work, perhaps for shorter hours or on a part-time basis in their old surroundings, perhaps by developing a hobby or interest into a second career. More and more often I see retired people running for public office or accepting consultative positions in public service.

Humility is a quality which can contribute much to a happy old age. The person who will not accept the slowing up which comes inevitably as the years pass, will often refuse to undertake even what he can do, because he cannot outtalk or outwork or outfight all his fellows as he once could. It is a great thing to know yourself, to be able to pace yourself. Though here too people differ. I know a woman of seventy-two who will still work all night without seeming to suffer for it, if she is doing something that really interests her.

But I did not begin this study to find hints for growing old happily. The secret of a happy life is the same in old age as it is in youth, and it is a paradoxical one. You find it by not looking for it.

There are things I want to do that I have never found time for. I should like to find time for them now. I would like to tie off knots in the things I have been doing, and hand them over to others. They will have to take charge of them sooner or later anyway. If I haven't woven a good thread it will fray quickly, but no matter how good it is it will fray in the end. Joys and sorrows and achievements and failures have their time, as we do, and then they pass away. We cannot revive them. We move on to another phase in life.

If we are open of mind and heart, if we have learned to accept life, we will know when one phase has ended and it is time for another to begin. If we are well-integrated and have faith in a Power greater than ourselves, we will enjoy each new phase and see it as a contribution to the whole as planned.

It has often seemed to me that spring and autumn are the most interesting seasons of the year because they are seasons of transition. Periodically among the ages also, there are periods of transition, dark ages and renaissances. Wouldn't it be interesting if we were now going through one of the ages of transition, perhaps from the Age of Materialism to the Age of the Spirit? Isn't it something worth thinking about? For if it happens it will be brought about by human thought and not by legislation.

An age of change is for the old or the young, those in the spring or the autumn of life, those in the seasons of change. The young bring eagerness and energy; the old bring strength for the hard pull. The young bring ideas and passions; the old bring patience and judgement. Life is a thrilling and exciting experience at any age, and by using it rightly we can be our own greatest achievement and source of ultimate content.

Mistletoe

This is the sacred golden bough whereunder
Died the Arician king; dark Hoder's dart,
It struck sun-singing Balder to a heart
Proof against stone and iron, in fatal blunder;
This is the self-sustaining tree of wonder
With golden knife cut by the Druid priest
To celebrate his great midwinter feast,
An innocent lightning and a silent thunder.

O clinging strength! O victory in defeat!
The winter-vanquished sun, ever resurgent,
Gleams on your greenness, berry-starred above;
Pagan and Christian here unwitting meet,
Their fading myths in fairer creed emergent,
As the kiss of peace proclaims the law of love.

Footnotes

1. "The World": Henry Vaughan.
2. "Adonais": Percy Bysshe Shelley.
3. Paraphrase of Psalm XC: Isaac Watts.
4. "The Garden of Proserpine": Algernon Charles Swinburne.
5. "Lucinda Matlock" in "Spoon River Anthology": Edgar Lee Masters.
   The quotation should read
   "Degenerate sons and daughters,
   Life is too strong for you —
   It takes life to love life:"
6. Psalm XC. The quotation should read:
   "A thousand years in Thy sight are but
   as yesterday when it is past, and as
   a watch in the night."
7. John X, 10. The quotation should read:
   "I am come that they might have life, and that they
   might have it more abundantly."
8. "Ulysses": Alfred, Lord Tennyson.
9. "The Difficult Art of Giving: The Epic of Alan Gregg": Wilder Penfield, O.M., M.D., F.R.S., Little Brown, 1967, p. 246.
10. "Ramon y Caja" in "The Second Career": Wilder Penfield, O.M., M.D., F.R.S., Little Brown, 1963, p. 85.
11. "The Difficult Art . . .", *sup. cit.*, p. 247.
12. *Ibid.*, p. 234.
13. *Ibid.*, p. 245.
14. *Ibid.*, p. 264.
15. "The Second Career", title essay in *op. sup. cit.*, pp. 10-11.
16. *Ibid.*, pp. 11-12.
17. *Ibid.*, pp. 15-16.
18. *Ibid.*, p. 16.
19. "Mankind in the Atomic Age" in "The Second Career", *sup. cit.*, p. 178.
20. "Neurosurgery—Yesterday, Today and Tomorrow", in "The Second Career", *sup. cit.*, p. 167.
21. "The Chief": Thomas Van Dusen, McGraw Hill, 1968, pp. 69-71.
22. "Renegade in Power": Peter C. Newman, McClelland and Stewart, 1963, p. 17.
23. "Canadian Born" in "Flint and Feather": Pauline Johnson, Musson.

24. "Renegade in Power", *sup. cit.*, p. 20.
25. *Ibid.*, p. 25.
26. "Mayor of all the People": Nathan Phillips, Q.C., McClelland and Stewart, p. 123.
27. *Ibid.*, p. 21.
28. *Ibid.*, p. 51.
29. *Ibid.*, p. 51.
30. *Ibid.*, p. 89.
31. *Ibid.*, p. 65.
32. *Ibid.*, p. 149.
33. *Ibid.*
34. "Une femme chez les hommes": Thérèse-F. Casgrain, Editions du Jour, 1971, p. 31.
    The original French edition of Mme. Casgrain's autobiography has been used to preserve the authentic nuances of feeling, and because, in a supposedly bilingual country, so distinguished a woman should be heard in her own voice and not through a translator.
35. "Le pays", 31 mai, 1913, in *op. cit.*, p. 46.
36. *Op. cit.*, p. 47.
37. "L'Habitant de Saint-Justin", Mémoires de la Société Royale du Canada, 2me Série, in *op. cit.*, p. 19.
38. *Ibid.*, p. 72.
39. *Ibid.*
40. "Ask no Quarter": Margaret Stewart and Doris French, Longmans Green, 1959.
41. *Ibid.*, p. 233.
42. *Ibid.*
43. "The Human Seasons": John Keats.
44. "The Hill": Rupert Brooke.
45. "Ask no Quarter", *sup. cit.*, p. 82.
46. *Ibid.*, p. 30.
47. "Une femme . . .", *sup. cit.*, p. 25.
48. *Ibid.*, p. 197.
49. "A Song in Storm": Rudyard Kipling.
50. "The Two Jungle Books": Rudyard Kipling, Macmillan, London, 1924, pp. 398-401.
51. "Paul-Emile, Cardinal Léger": Bernard Murchland, Univ. of Notre Dame Press, p. 7.
52. "Moral Essays" (Epistle III, 1. 96): Alexander Pope.
53. Murchland, *op. cit.*, p. 13.
54. *Ibid.*, p. 14.
55. *Ibid.*, p. 16.
56. *Ibid.*, p. 21.
57. *Ibid.*, p. 22.
58. *Ibid.*, pp. 40-44.
59. James Russell Lowell.
60. "Weekend Magazine", Aug. 16, 1969.
61. *Ibid.*

62. *Ibid.*
63. "Toronto Star", Apr. 22, 1972.
64. *Ibid.*
65. "Weekend Magazine", Aug. 16. 1969.
66. Thomas Nelson & Sons.
67. The Perkins Bull Foundation, George J. McLeod.
68. "From Hummingbird to Eagle": Wm. Perkins Bull, Q.C., LL.D., p. 15.
69. "Ryerson", 168, pp. 18-23.
70. Wm. Perkins Bull, *op. cit.*, p. 186. This was doubtless the female mentioned on p. 8 of Mr. Ivor's own book.
71. "I Live with Birds": Roy Ivor, Ryerson, 1968, Foreword by Hugh M. Halliday, pp. vi-vii.
72. *Ibid.*, p. 20.
73. *Ibid.*
74. Jan. 27, 1973.
75. "September Gale": John A. R. McLeish, Dent, 1955, p. 194.
76. "A Painter's Country": A. Y. Jackson, Clarke Irwin, 1958, pp. 131-2.
77. *Ibid.*
78. *Ibid.*, p. 34.
79. McLeish, *op. cit.*, p. 25.
80. *Ibid.*, pp. 44-5.
81. *Ibid.*, p. 74-5.
82. *Ibid.*, p. 79.
83. Jackson, *op. cit.*, p. 93.
84. *Ibid.*
85. McLeish, *op. cit.*, pp. 88-93.
86. *Ibid.*
87. Jackson, *op. cit.*, p. 146.
88. 1957.
89. "Mitchell Hepburn": Neil McKenty, McClelland and Stewart, p. 104.
90. *Ibid.*
91. *Ibid.*, p. 115.
92. "Saturday Night", May 23, 1953.
93. Dr. McClure says only that his own blood was compatible with that of the patient to whom he gave a transfusion on his own operating-table.
94. "Maclean's Magazine", Dec., 1968.
95. "Toronto Star", Nov. 27, 1971.
96. "Maclean's Magazine", Dec., 1968.
97. "Abou Ben Adhem": Leigh Hunt. Abou had a vision of an angel writing "the names of those that love the Lord". Abou's not being among them, he said to the angel: "I pray thee then Write me as one that loves his fellow men." The angel returned next night to show Abou the list of "those whom love of God had blest, And lo! Ben Adhem's name led all the rest."
98. "Dictionary of Canadian Biography", Macmillan.
99. "Maclean's Magazine", Sept. 17, 1966.
100. In "Ottawa Journal", Feb. 24, 1969.
101. Introduction by General Vanier to "Man and his Family": Wilder Penfield, McClelland and Stewart, p. 8.

102. *Ibid.*
103. "My Very Good Dear Friends": Chief Dan George, in "The Only Good Indian", ed. Waubageshbig, New Press.
104. "Time", Feb. 15, 1971.
105. *See* note 103.
106. "Speech to the Canadian Council of Christians and Jews": Chief Dan George.
107. *Ibid.*
109. "Cross Country", Collins, 1949.
110. *Ibid.*
111. "A Defence of Poetry": Percy Bysshe Shelley.
112. "Two Solitudes": Hugh MacLennan, Macmillan, 1945, p. 281.
113. *Ibid.*, p. 315.
114. *Ibid.*, p. 317.
115. "Cross Country" (title essay), p. 81.
116. "Michael."